Time-Slips

Journeys into the Past

and the Future

Rodney Davies

Also by Rodney Davies

Non Fiction

Journeys to Heaven and to Hell

Balm From Beyond

Disembodied Voices

The Lazarus Syndrome

Doubles: The Enigma of the Second Self

Supernatural Disappearances

Dowsing: Ancient Origins and Modern Uses

Personal Secrets

Sensual Secrets

The Zodiac Guide to Living

The ESP Workbook

Fiction

The Man Who Made Coffins

Time-Slips

Journeys into the Past and the Future

Rodney Davies

Published by Beccles Books Ltd
1 Exchange House, Exchange Square
Beccles, Suffolk NR34 9HH

First published in 2019
ISBN 9781795026970

Cover Picture by Roz Charles

CONTENTS

List of Illustrations

INTRODUCTION

THE PHENOMENON OF TIME

Down in the earth, in dark, alone,
A mockery of the ghost in bone,
The strangeness, passing the unknown.

From *The Passing Strange* by John Masefield

We are all time travellers, or at least we are after a fashion. I myself have seemingly journeyed more than half a century into the future since the day of my birth, and everybody else has made a similar apparent forward movement in time, whose length mirrors our respective ages. We will not only carry on doing so until our eyes close for the last time, but we will continue to do so after death; indeed, the atoms making up our dead bodies will remain in existence long after their dissolution by decay or by incineration, and they will thereafter be re-cycled a countless number of times until the end of the universe, when time, as we call it, comes to a stop. The same is true for all other living things and for inanimate objects, both in this world and elsewhere.

We categorise this 'passing strange' phenomenon called time as the fourth dimension. The first three dimensions, those of length, breadth and height, are the spatial extensions of matter; time, by contrast, arises from them, for it is nothing other than the measure of their -- or matter's -- change. Matter by its nature is unstable, constantly breaking down and recombining, and the rate at which such changes occur, when compared together, comprises time.

There is no time, therefore, in a vacuum, and neither is there any without consciousness, for time is essentially a mental concept based on comparison. If all change could be suddenly stopped, time would simultaneously vanish without trace, and everything would be held in a static limbo, much like figures in a photograph. Nobody, I think, would wish to be thus preserved, although because all our mental processes would presumably be likewise arrested, we would not know that anything odd had happened to us.

But time, according to our everyday experience of it, has the perverse habit of moving only in one direction, thereby continually hustling us along, much to our chagrin, from birth to death. As a tombstone epitaph remarks: 'Time, like an ever-flowing stream, bears all our loves away'. In this regard it simply reflects the physics and chemistry of matter, although its apparently irreversible one-way flow contrasts with the nature of the three other dimensions, all of which can be changed -- made smaller or larger -- to some degree at least.

We divide time into three parts: the past, which has already happened; the present, which we are currently experiencing; and the future, which is yet to come. We often look back at the past with either nostalgia or regret, and forward to the future with either hope or trepidation, and while we accept that we cannot alter what has gone before, we can derive some comfort from the fact that, by acting sensibly and opportunely today, we may be able to organise the future to our satisfaction and advantage. The only problem with 'the future' is that we never reach it, for all our experiences take place in the present; it is therefore like the mirage of a desert oasis that stays tantalisingly distant no matter how long the hot and thirsty explorers tramp towards it.

The past has a similar unreal quality to it. Everything that took place in our lives before this moment lies in the past, yet when those events happened to us they did so in 'the present'. After all, on this date and hour in 2010, or whatever earlier year of life we may care to choose, we neither thought that we were living in the future, which it was compared with previous years, nor in the past, which it is compared with now. Rather, it was the present, one different of course from what we are currently experiencing, but none the less in essence exactly the same. And although the past is made more tangible by us having lived through the experiences that comprise it, and by our memories and other mementoes of it, we are seemingly as powerless to return to it and perhaps do things differently, as we are of leaping ahead into what we call tomorrow.

Hence is time, therefore, something that is passing by and hurrying us along with it, or is its passage apparent rather than real? The turning of our planet and its journey around the sun provide us with the two most important natural measurements of time -- the day and the year -- but what is being measured? We say that the days and years are passing by and will continue to do so *ad infinitum*, thereby marking out the past, the present, and the future, but might we not equally claim that such markers are nothing more than the attendant effects of planetary rotation in a continuous present, and that we are mistaking alternating days and nights, and indeed the seasons, for *evolving* days and nights and seasons, thereby creating something that does not in reality exist, namely time?

Picture how different things would seem to us if the Earth's axis was vertical rather than inclined and if our planet turned only once about its axis as it orbited the sun. This would cause the same hemisphere to face sunwards, giving it continual daylight, while the other hemisphere would remain wrapped in Stygian gloom. Neither would experience any obvious seasonal changes; indeed, the sunlit side would be uncomfortably hot, except at its margins, and the dark side frozen solid.

Anyone living on the latter might notice that the starry constellations were shifting very slowly across the sky, and they would see the moon make a faster, but none the less still slow, regularly repeated journey across it, which might give them an idea of passing time. Those living on the sunny side, however, would have no such obvious clues. The stars would be invisible to them, and the sun would remain in the same position in the sky. In case you might think that the inhabitants of both planetary halves, if any, would surely have to sleep, so giving them alternating periods of consciousness and unconsciousness, which would suggest a passage of time, it is relevant to note that we and other animals only sleep because there are nights to sleep in; without nights, sleep might not have evolved, or if it did it would probably be erratic and unregulated.

There are two models, I believe, which can be used to portray the relationship of the present to 'the past' and to 'the future'. The first is the train carriage model, and the second is the film strip model. Both demonstrate how the past, the present, and the future are actually the same thing. Yet the first suggests time travel is impossible, the second that it is possible, which reflects the enigmatic nature of time.

To understand the train carriage model, which exactly mimics everyday experience, we must imagine ourselves seated aboard the carriage of a train standing at a platform in station A. We are waiting for the train to depart and travel along the railway line to station B, our destination. We are of course in the present, whereas our journey and our arrival at station B lie in the future.

Suddenly, the station master blows his whistle and the train sets off, soon leaving station A behind. We are still in the present, but station A and the various occurrences that happened to us there have become part of the past, while our arrival at station B still lies in the future. As the train picks up speed it runs over more and more track, whose location *vis-à-vis* ourselves also becomes part of the past, like those activities we were engaged in -- talking, drinking coffee, reading, sleeping, etc. -- at the time. Similarly, the length of track in front of the train shortens as we near our destination, and indeed it isn't long before the train pulls into station B, where our journey ends.

But while we have accomplished something that was set in the future when we were at station A, we have remained continually in the present, whereas station A and all that took place there has apparently become part of the past. Yet when we were at station A, we knew that it, as well as station B and the railway track linking them (despite the fact that they were out of our view), all existed in the present we were experiencing then, just as they were throughout our journey, and that they remained so even when we arrived at station B.

Thus in this model, the past and the future are merely terms for activities and incidents that once were, where the past is concerned, or which will be, where the future is concerned, in our consciousness. Yet neither exists as a separate entity, which is why we could not travel through time to visit them. For although we can, for example, return to station A, doing so would not mean we were travelling back in time. Indeed, the intention of going there automatically places our arrival in the future, and when we arrived we would find ourselves where we have been all along, in the present.

In the second, or film-strip model, we must imagine ourselves sitting in a cinema watching a movie. The images that are being projected on to the screen before us represent 'the present' in the film story that is unfolding, while those that we have already seen form 'the past', and those that are to come, 'the future' Yet we know that the film-strip exists along with ourselves in the present, and that the past and the future where it is concerned are nothing more than the products of its linear passage through the lens aperture of the projector, and hence, as in the train carriage model, result from position. Yet unlike the train carriage model, those past and future events have an objective reality, despite being out of view.

If he wished, the projectionist could re-wind the film and show us 'the past' again, although those scenes would, when shown, simultaneously become 'the present'. Or he could run it ahead and show us scenes that lie in 'the future', which we would not otherwise see for another hour or so, and which would then become 'the present' to us when projected on to the screen. He could even, if the film was wound on to three spools and if I visited the projection room, show me scenes from the end of the film, while you're still watching the action in the middle. We would both be in 'the present', although the film scenes I was viewing, which would constitute part of my present, would be situated, from your point of view, in 'the future'.

Hence 'time travel' where the film-strip is concerned is possible, although we are not really travelling in time, due to the fact that the whole of the film story, as I mentioned above, exists in 'the present'. We are instead occupying different viewing positions, which correspond to the start or to the end of the film, or to somewhere in between.

As members of the film audience we can only see and hear what is on the screen and must remember what has already been shown, and try to guess at how the plot will develop and the film end. But this is identical to the situation in which we find ourselves in life. We are aware of the present moment and have a memory of what has gone before, although we can only surmise how the remainder of our lives (or even tomorrow) will turn out. Hence like the film passing through the light beam in order to have its images projected on to a cinema screen, our conscious awareness may be travelling along an already completed circuit or course, one formed by each of our lives and the events associated with them. If so, our lives wholly occupy, in the same way that a reel of film does, the present, yet they appear to be divided into a past and a future as well, due to the fact that consciousness is wafer thin and only regards what it is directly aware of as 'the present' or now.

This film-strip model, unlike the railway carriage model, makes it possible for 'the future' -- with regard to the activities of the people in the film as opposed to those in the railway carriage -- to be predicted, and it explains the apparent immutability of fate, for everything already exists in the present; and it allows for time travel, if we can call it that, to occur.

In the following chapters I shall consider many cases of people who have had what is called a time-slip, whereby they have found themselves in either 'the past' or 'the future', a displacement that can likewise affect other organisms, as well as non-living things, which will hopefully persuade you that 'time travel' can and does happen; that such time-slips take place spontaneously and do not require a complicated technology to effect; and that, while of comparatively rare occurrence, they are frequent enough to deserve serious attention, not least because by acknowledging and accepting that such marvels are possible, it allows our minds to scale the walls of scepticism and disdain which our scientific culture erects around them, thereby freeing consciousness sufficiently to prompt them into being.

And if that sounds paradoxical, then welcome to the strange world of time!

CHAPTER ONE

MOVEMENTS IN TIME

The bird of god descends between two moments
Like silence into music, opening a way through time.

From *Air* by Kathleen Raine

There are many cases on record which describe how a person has suddenly and unexpectedly found himself or herself in another time. Occasionally, two or more people may undergo such a time-slip together. The experience is usually quite short and seldom has an obvious purpose. It rarely involves any sensation of physical movement; indeed, the person (or people) concerned is usually quite unaware that anything strange has happened until he or she views or even meets the differently-dressed inhabitants or encounters some unusual, incongruous scene, which alerts him to the fact. And likewise, his or her return to what he or she regards as 'the present' is equally rapid and sudden. Yet the ease and smoothness of such a time-slip is perhaps not so surprising if the past and the future, as the last chapter suggested, actually coexist with the present yet cannot normally be observed.

Most time-slips, but by no means all, result in someone being 'taken back' into the past. This has led some sceptics to claim that the event is therefore a subjective phenomenon, resulting from the imagination interacting with a previously acquired knowledge of the past, the two bubbling and fizzing together to produce an hallucinatory scene that seems real, but which of course is not. Yet the typical subject of a time-slip is a non-anxious, psychologically stable individual, of the type least likely to have an hallucination, and who undergoes the experience only once, which is most unusual for a mental aberration. And he or she invariably has no particular knowledge of the historical scene or event witnessed.

Similarly, when two or more people are involved, their subsequent accounts of what they experienced are typically either exactly or essentially the same. This, too, points to it being a shared objective experience, as it is unlikely, if not impossible, for two or more people to simultaneously hallucinate the same scene.

The distances travelled forwards or backwards in time vary considerably. Sometimes the time-slip is comparatively short in length, involving a movement, if we may call it that, of a few hours, days or weeks, or occasionally a few years. Such short time-slips are typical of those made into the future, while those which take people into the past can be considerably longer; not only have backward journeys of centuries and even millennia been reported, but there is evidence to suggest that huge backward time-slips of many millions of years have been made.

Now while this book is devoted mainly to the sudden translocation of people into tomorrow or yesterday, we cannot ignore the fact that other animals and also plants, as well as non-living objects, may be similarly whisked away. The objects which go missing, or which at least are believed to go missing, in this manner are typically small commonplace man-made articles, like pieces of jewellery, spectacles, coins, keys, rings, etc., even though on occasions larger and more unusual manufactured items may be similarly transported. Natural objects like stones and twigs may also be time-shifted, yet because their vanishing from today is seldom noticed and because they are rarely recognised as being new arrivals in the place to which they are taken, their identification as time-slipped objects is usually overlooked.

It goes without saying that if a person, animal or object is wholly time-slipped, he, she or it will vanish from the present in a way that seems supernatural. Indeed, readers of my book *Supernatural Disappearances* will know that there are many cases of such remarkable vanishings on record, and they may perhaps recall that these can be grouped into three main categories.

The first consists of those supernatural disappearances

which are not followed by the return of what vanishes, so that he, she or it is seemingly lost for ever; the second comprises those disappearances where the subject vanishes at one place and immediately reappears at another and often distant place, while the third involves a person, animal or object that supernaturally disappears but then equally mysteriously reappears after an interval of time has gone by, either at the same spot or at another, sometimes distant, place.

The last category certainly involves a time-slip, for the subject is evidently taken into 'the future', and does not rematerialize until that moment of time becomes what we call 'the present'. Such a time-slip may also happen to whatever supernaturally vanishes but does not reappear, which presumably would happen if the subject was transported back into the past or moved so far into the future that the moment of his, her or its reappearance has not yet occurred. However, objects which are taken back into the past may sometimes turn up again, most noticeably in rock strata, where they occur as anomalous fossils, so revealing that they were shifted backwards by tens or even hundreds of millions of years.

The short forward time-slip, whereby typically an object mysteriously vanishes only to reappear equally mysteriously not long afterwards, happens quite frequently, even though it is usually explained by the happy subject assuming that the item was simply lost on the first occasion and found again on the second. The reader has probably experienced such a frustrating event himself without realising that a far more intriguing phenomenon took place than a straightforward loss.

A correspondent, David Gamon of Wells, in Somerset, wrote to me describing how this situation occurred in his own life, noting: 'I have lost far more pairs of underpants, single socks, and keys than my absence of mind will explain, and once a radio I had taken out of a car to put in the next one seemed to vanish from the cupboard I had put it in.'

David went on to add:

I have known keys to reappear; earlier this year a key

which had been in my pocket could not be found. Now, my habit is every night to take off our dog's harness and put it on a chair in the corner of our kitchen, then pick it up to dress her again in that the next morning . . . and one morning this key was on top of the harness as if it had rematerialized there.

Another example of this puzzling sort of thing, which may also have involved a short forward time-slip, was recorded by Hereward Carrington in the December, 1930 edition of the *Journal* of the American Society for Psychical Research. It perplexed the nurse to whom it happened, the methodical Miss K., who always laid her bunch of keys on the dining room table when she returned home to her apartment:

> One day she did this (so she declares) and, a short time afterwards, looked for them, as she was about to leave the apartment on another "case". Her keys had disappeared. She looked for them everywhere; they were not to be found. She finally had to have other keys made for the front door, etc. Several days later, she wished to get a cork for a medicine bottle, having broken the old one. These corks were kept in a tin box, in the bottom partition of a trunk, standing in the hall. She does not (she said) have occasion to open this drawer more than three or four times a year. There, in the tin box, was her bunch of keys. Miss K. declared most emphatically that she did not open this drawer on the day in question, nor subsequently until she looked for the cork. Nevertheless, her keys were there, peacefully reposing in the tin box.

If the nurse accurately reported what happened, and we have no reason to suppose that she did not, then her keys were certainly supernaturally shifted from her dining room table into the tin box lying at the bottom partition of the trunk, which is of course incredible enough in itself, and they may also have been shifted forward in time by an interval of the few days that passed before she looked in the box, although we cannot know how long the time-slip, if one occurred, really was.

The next example also comes from the other side of the Atlantic, but this time from Canada, and it was told to the psychic researcher A.R.G. Owen in the early 1970s by the Toronto woman to whom it happened. If the facts are as Owen presents them, then the incident not only involves a definite time-slip, but also one which took the object in question -- a small plastic 45 rpm child's record -- about five years into the future.

Now one day the woman had been changing the nappy of her one-year-old son on the living room table. The baby was clasping the aforementioned toy record, which he loved to bite into and which bore his teeth marks. Then quite suddenly, the fractious infant threw the record up into the air, and to the woman's absolute astonishment it literally vanished right before her eyes. Flabbergasted, and doubting what she had seen, she quickly set about looking for it, a task which eventually had her moving the furniture and even turning back the carpets, but without her finding the disc anywhere.

Five years then passed, during which period the living room was redecorated and the furniture changed, yet the record that had so suddenly disappeared remained both absent and a continuing mystery. Then one evening, while the woman was awaiting the arrival of a couple of dinner guests, she went to her record player intending to put on some light music. She lifted the machine's lid -- and inside, she was stunned to see, lying on the turn-table, with the impressions of her now six-year-old son's baby teeth marks very much in evidence, was the toy record that had vanished all those years before!

She could not explain how it got there. It certainly had not been in the record player for five years, for the machine had been used many times during that period, and her son insisted he had not found the record and put it there. And her second child, then a two-year-old girl, was too small to reach and open the record player, even if she had come across the record in, say, a crack between the floorboards. Likewise, the woman's mother, who frequently baby-sat the two children, and who knew all about the record and its unaccountable disappearance, vigorously denied having found it and put it on the record turn-table; indeed, because she was as interested as her daughter in solving the mystery, she would not have added to it by placing the record there, even if she had found it.

The toy record may therefore have vanished in mid-air as it appears to have done, and then been moved forward by time-slip five years, to rematerialize and come to rest on the record turn-table, so enabling it to be found by the woman that day when she lifted the record player's lid.

If this is what happened, then the event had no apparent purpose to it, other than perhaps opening the woman's eyes to such oddities. But we should not expect occurrences like this to necessarily have a purpose if they can happen spontaneously, as most such events will doubtlessly only take place when the conditions are somehow right for them to occur, and therefore they will lack what we call 'meaning'.

Although an object may, like the disappearing record, be seen to vanish, the opposite may occur -- that is, the object may be lost in what appears to be a normal way but then suddenly materialize out of thin air at a later date. When this happens we can be fairly sure that the object underwent a time-slip, particularly if it manifests at a distant site and is lacking any deposit or mark to suggest it had remained at the place where it was lost until the moment of its return.

Such a time-slip brought back the signet ring which accidentally fell from the finger of author and mystic Wellesley Tudor Pole, when he reached out for a loose rope while steering a felucca up the Nile towards Cairo in November 1918, and which dropped into the depths of the muddy river. The signet ring had been given to Pole, who was then a Major in the British Army, earlier that year when he was stationed at Haifa, in Israel, by the Bahai leader Abdul Baha Abbas, whose protection he had organised. It was inscribed in Persian with the names and titles of God, and had been specially blessed by Abdul Baha, which made it a much valued gift. Indeed, Pole was so distressed by its loss that he prayed each day thereafter for its recovery.

His prayers were not only answered, but he was reunited

with the ring in a most unusual way about three months later, near the end of February 1919, when he was seated at his office desk in the British Military HQ in Cairo:

> Suddenly a shot rang out (Pole writes) apparently fired from a balcony across the street. The bullet missed me by two feet or so and embedded itself in the wall facing the window. At that very moment my ring fell down upon the blotter on the desk in front of me with a sharp thud. It was intact in every way and is still in my possession.

The ring had not only materialised out of thin air in front of the startled Major Pole, but it had been teleported into his office a couple of miles from the site of its loss in the river Nile. Yet equally remarkably, because it lacked any form of aquatic accretion and still retained its original glitter, the ring had seemingly also been shifted forward in time, so that it reappeared in 'the present' of Major Pole three months later just as it was when he lost it. However, it is also possible that the ring, on the day of its loss, may have been transferred to, and held in, another dimension of being, until it was supernaturally reintroduced into our world and fell on to Pole's blotter.

Coincidentally, shortly before the ring, which fitted loosely, had slipped from his finger into the Nile, Major Pole had been shot at from a nearby island by an earlier would-be assassin, who had also missed him. Indeed, the conditions at the time of the ring's loss were remarkably similar, as he himself noted, to those pertaining when it was returned to him:

'The hour of the day, the weather, and the transit of the bullet were all repeated, the main difference being of course that the loss took place in the water and in the open air, and the recovery took place on land and in a room.'

This might mean that the similar conditions played a part in bringing about the return of the ring, by perhaps forming a focus for its forward movement in time.

The idea that an object which supernaturally disappears may be held in some type of limbo until it equally

14

enigmatically returns at a later date is suggested by the 'lost apple' experience of Alan Mayne, a member of the Society for Psychical Research. The incident, which is very similar to the previous two, happened, as far as Alan could remember, sometime between 1956 and 1959, when he occupied a bed-sit in Divinity Road, Oxford.

One evening there, feeling somewhat peckish, Alan picked up a pale green apple to eat, but as he was in the process of conveying it to his mouth in order to bite a piece from it, it unfortunately slipped from his grasp and fell to the floor with an audible 'plop'. He immediately set about trying to find where it had bounced and rolled to, but the search, like that for the aforementioned 45-rpm record, was completely unsuccessful. Alan hunted all around the room, looking in every nook and cranny, but the apple, much to his chagrin and bafflement, was nowhere to be found. 'This seemed to me,' he noted, 'like a definite disappearance, as it was verified by the fact that the apple did not turn up later on, nor was there any smell of decaying apple.'

That was how things remained until one day 'considerably later' when Alan went to dinner with a friend, Dr. Winifred Leyshan, a retired teacher of physics, who was, he says, 'well-trained for careful observation, and not in any way given to fanciful explanation, though she was open-minded about the existence of psychic phenomena'. Neither had she been told about the green apple which had so mysteriously vanished in Alan's bed-sitting room.

The meal was eaten at the kitchen table, and was just about completed, when to their astonishment, Alan Mayne recounted, 'a small *wizened* green apple suddenly dropped on to my plate,' which caused Dr Leyshan to gasp and exclaim, 'Could it be a poltergeist?' Alan said that he first saw 'the wizened apple at about eye level, and when it arrived on the plate it did not roll around, which suggests a relatively soft landing'.

Alan remarks that the kitchen window was open at the top at the time, but claims that if the apple had arrived by being thrown through the gap it could not possibly have made such a graceful vertical descent on to his plate. He was also looking at Dr Leyshan immediately beforehand, and had she tried to play a silly trick on him he would not have missed seeing her toss the apple up into the air.

The sudden appearance of a green apple, albeit a wizened one, dropping out of the air on to Alan's plate, just as Wellesley Pole's lost signet ring had fallen equally dramatically on to his desk in front of him, suggests that it was the same apple which had gone AWOL in his bed-sitting room. If it *was* the same one, then we can perhaps conclude that following its vanishing, the apple was held in some sort of limbo wherein it aged and withered, just as it would have done had it remained unfound in Alan's bed-sit. The same 'holding' may also have happened to Wellesley Pole's ring, although because a ring cannot deteriorate as speedily as a living apple, there were no obvious signs that it had been.

The fact that the apple came back in a wizened state was, from its point of view, to its advantage, for it meant that Alan Mayne would no longer wish to eat it. Its return in someone else's house also diminished that possibility, as did its arrival back right after he'd finished eating his dinner there, when he must have been quite full up, rather than doing so sometime before. This looks very much as if the apple perfectly timed its reappearance to avoid suffering the fate of being bitten into that it had so luckily avoided in Alan's bed-sit.

If this sounds fanciful, it should be remembered that apples, other fruits and vegetables, and plants in general, do not like being eaten, despite their seeming acquiescence to the procedure. Indeed, it has been known since the 1960s -- when Cleve Backster discovered that his potted *Dracaena* plant (suitably wired to a galvanometer) quailed with alarm, trembled and then 'fainted' with shock, not just when actually harmed but when mentally threatened with harm -- that plants are sensitive and perceptive organisms, which suffer quite as much as do animals when handled roughly or treated unkindly, or when they are tortured by being boiled, fried, grilled, baked or eaten alive. Hence if Alan's apple vanished when it was filled with fear, this emotion may have helped retain it in the beyond until it was no longer at all tempting to his palate.

These various examples, some of which feature a non-living object being apparently time-slipped into the future, share a common characteristic in that the items concerned remain somehow linked with, and are returned to, their owners and/or the places where they were kept, who or which seemingly acted as a 'return focus' for them.

Most of those that time-slip in people's homes remain in those homes, although they come back in a different place. The missing record turned up at a site that was particularly appropriate for it, the gramophone turn-table, like the key lost by Mr Gamon of Wells, who could not help noticing it on his dog's harness, but the nurse's keys, oddly enough, did not. Wellesley Tudor Pole's ring dropped out of the air in front of him when the conditions in his office approximated to those where it was lost. The distance between that spot and his office was about two miles, which suggests that the reappearance of an object undergoing a time-slip, and thus the length of the time-slip itself, may sometimes be determined by the owner (the primary return focus) placing himself in conditions similar to those at the place of its disappearance, thereby creating a return focus with the necessary energies to rematerialize the object.

The missing green apple, although 'lost' in Alan Mayne's bed-sit, was remarkably returned to a completely different location -- someone else's house -- while he was having dinner there. It reunited itself with him, we might say, as its primary return focus, but it did so when (and where) it was least likely to be eaten, which perhaps means that an apple, despite its seeming lack of personality and intelligence, can somehow organise its own protection if circumstances allow.

It is of course difficult to regard objects which have vanished on one day and turned up again on another as having travelled in time, because we are in 'the present' on both occasions. And because the present we occupy on the day of the object's return is 'now' to us, the object which vanished two or three days earlier (or whenever) is more likely to be regarded as coming from the past, than reaching the end of a time slip into 'the future'. Such strangeness again suggests that time is not divisible into past, present and future, but consists instead of a continuous present within which those moments that are somehow selectively illuminated by our consciousness we mistakenly insist on calling 'now'.

Yet the Oneness or Eternal Present contains everything that has ever been or will be, including the whole of your life and mine, metaphorically stretching behind and beyond us, silent and unseen, and which lies behind a curtain so fine that, when the conditions are somehow right for it to be breached, an object like a bunch of keys or a chewed record, or even the occasional startled person, can pass harmlessly and effortlessly through it into what we call 'the past' or 'the future'.

This strange time curtain was momentarily drawn back in the mid-1960s alongside a Southampton botany student named Michael Higgins, when he took a day's outing to do some field study at Old Winchester Hill. As he drove through the Meon Valley, having taken a minor road leading up a low incline, he had a fine view out over the surrounding countryside towards Hambledon, which reminded him of its cricketing associations.

Then at that moment he suddenly saw several people, animals and non-living things, from 'the past'. For on the other side of the road, travelling in the same direction that he was but which he was overtaking, he caught sight of four horses pulling a coach. He had time as he passed them to notice the coachman driving the vehicle, the man sitting beside him, and another man at its rear who held a post horn. All were dressed in old-fashioned clothes, which prompted Michael to assume that a film was probably being shot. Yet when he reached the top of the hill and was able to stop the car, alight from it, and look round at the scene, he saw that there was no sign of a coach and horses or track-way anywhere, and certainly no film crew, but only an empty grassy field.

But although this sudden and remarkable sighting appeared to be, from Michael's point of view, the brief intrusion of objects, animals and people from 'the past' into his present, it is perhaps better described as a temporary merging of two presents, the coach and four and those aboard it belonging to a 'past present', while the surrounding landscape and Michael's car belonged to 'the present' he was then experiencing.

A similar meeting with a horse drawn vehicle that vanished is described by Andrew Lang in his book *Dreams and Ghosts*, which was first published in 1897. The strange encounter happened in the New Forest to a man named Hyndford while he rode from his residence there towards a town several miles away, but which Lang, for some reason, does not name. Arriving at a grassy glade, Mr Hyndford, who is described by Lang as being 'a distinguished and accomplished country gentleman and politician, of scientific tastes,' suddenly noticed a carriage passing by on the other side of the bushes at its border, which came into full and clear view as the equipage passed a gap between them. The vehicle was an old-fashioned family carriage with imitation wicker work sides 'on green panel which were once so common', pulled by two horses, whose driver was recognisably a family servant. Seated in the carriage were two elderly ladies, one of whom wore a hat, the other a bonnet.

As the carriage went out of sight again, Mr Hyndford rode through the gap in pursuit of it, hoping that he might obtain directions from the driver, but to his absolute astonishment he found that there was no sign of the carriage and its occupants, that the avenue they appeared to have been following ended in a thick, impenetrable growth of bracken forming a *cul-de-sac*, and that the grass over which the carriage was travelling bore no sign of the imprint of horse shoes, scuff marks or indeed wheel tracks. So what had appeared to be so real and tangible to Mr Hyndford moments before had completely disappeared in the time it took for him to pass through the opening in pursuit. Moreover, being a person who knew that perceptions can sometimes be mistaken, he returned to the place where he had first noticed the carriage and looked for anything which might have suggested such a vehicle with its three occupants to him. Nothing of the kind, however, was in evidence. He therefore went on, totally baffled by what he had seen.

Andrew Lang attempts to explain Mr Hyndford's experience by calling it a 'subjective hallucination', despite the fact that all hallucinations, arising as they do spontaneously in the mind of the percipient, are *ipso facto* subjective. But it is difficult to understand why Mr Hyndford, any more than Michael Higgins, should hallucinate a horse-drawn vehicle bearing three people, even though such ensembles were common in the 19th century. There is no evidence that either man had had such a remarkable experience before or ever did again, which suggests that it was an actual sighting, not a mental fabrication. But what Mr Hyndford saw could likewise be explained by two times coming briefly together, so that the 'past present' occupied by the horse-drawn carriage with green sides merged with 'the present' he was experiencing, the two fleetingly uniting as one.

This would mean that the respective sightings, by both Mr Hyndford and the carriage's occupants, of each other were veridical experiences, and Mr Hyndford's sudden appearance would without doubt have been as strange and perplexing to the old ladies and their driver as they were to him, and as Michael Higgins and his car were to those in the coach and four.

CHAPTER TWO

DREAMING IN TIME

Here death may deal not again for ever;
Here change may come not till all change end

From *A Forsaken Garden* by Algernon Swinburne

The cases discussed in the previous chapter indicate that our traditional view of time as a river inexorably sweeping us along like flotsam from the past towards an unknown future is wrong. Time, in fact, has no existence outside ourselves; rather, its presence is suggested to us by the positional changes of physical objects around us, most notably those that occur regularly, like the earth's rotation which brings about the rising and setting of both the sun and the moon, and thus time's seeming reality. In this respect we resemble the prisoners in Plato's cave who mistook shadows for real things.

Indeed, what we call time is apparent only because our consciousness, informed as it is by our sense organs, is normally only aware of consecutive 'moments' in our lives, which we call 'the present'. This naturally suggests that if our consciousness could be widened, we would be able to view what we call 'the past' and 'the future' now, because both are as much 'now' as now is.

Such widening of consciousness does sometimes take place, which brings about what are called pre-cognitive (or 'known before') and retro-cognitive (or 'known afterwards') experiences. These happen most commonly when we are asleep, during dreams. For while many dreams are created by the sleeping mind as a way of visually addressing the various problems and difficulties which are causing us anxiety, some -- but perhaps no more than five to ten per cent of them --

show us either what lies ahead or take us 'back' into the sometimes distant past. This is when consciousness may even travel along the interlinking 'conduit' of our respective lives to perceive events which belong to a previous, or to a forthcoming existence. In most cases, however, the dream consciousness tends to be focused on 'looking ahead' to future events of this life.

Unfortunately, our sleeping minds often cannot 'look ahead' as clearly as we would like, so such dreams of the future may appear 'as through a glass, darkly', their contents distorted or expressed in symbolic form, whereby they make no immediate sense on waking to us. Help may therefore have to be sought from a professional diviner or from a dream book.

One familiar Biblical example of such a dream was that had by an Egyptian Pharaoh (whom some scholars believe was Akhenaten, the husband of Nefertiti), in which he saw seven fat kine or cattle coming up out of a river followed by seven lean kine, which ate up the first, and seven plump ears of corn growing on one stalk of wheat followed by seven thin ears, blasted by an east wind, which grew on another. The Pharaoh remained perplexed by the dream until Joseph, who evidently had an intuitive talent for dream interpretation, told him it meant his realm would enjoy seven years of plenty followed by seven years of famine, and that the latter period would therefore need preparing for, which, following Joseph's warning, is what was done.

A more recent and quite remarkable example of such a symbolic dream is recorded by John Beaumont in his *Treatise on Spirits, Apparitions, Witchcrafts and other Magical Practices*, published in 1705, and which is taken from a Latin account published almost two centuries earlier by Ioannis Pontanus. Beaumont writes,

> So Pontanus tells us, that a certain soldier of Genoa dreamt he was devoured by a Serpent, wherefore on a day, when the other soldiers were put on board ships to fight with the enemy, he kept himself at home; but a tumult casually arising in the city, he was killed by the ball of a sort of cannon, which we called a Serpent.

Although Beaumont says nothing about the cause of the attack on Genoa, it was probably that which the French king Louis XII (reigned 1462-1515) mounted in 1507, following a revolt by the Genoese against his rule.

But notwithstanding the symbolism in this case, when an event dreamed of occurs in the near future, a dream can often provide the sleeper with an exact sight of it. This is particularly true in those dreams which 'preview' the dreamer's own death or some other upsetting incident in which he or she, or a loved one, is the victim.

A tragic and touching example of such an unambiguous dream was had in January, 1844 by a young coal miner named John Gray, who worked at the Crump Meadow coal pit near Cinderford, in Gloucestershire, and who was the sole support of his widowed mother and his sister. At breakfast on the Monday in question, the young man told his mother that during the night he had dreamed of himself being killed in the pit by a large rock that fell on him. His mother, however, made somewhat light of the dream, and Gray, being half-persuaded by her, went off to work, although not without twice returning home to bid what he feared might be a 'last goodbye' to her.

And John Gray's dream proved correct, for upon having laboured underground for several hours, an enormous block of stone, which would take several men to move, suddenly tumbled from the gallery roof on to him, and crushed him, it was reported, 'in the most frightful manner'. The poor fellow lingered on in the most indescribable agony for just under an hour, until 'death released him from his sufferings'.

A similar foreshowing of the accident which led to the dreamer's own death, whose sad outcome took place even more quickly, was given to a young sailor aboard the London Merchant steam-ship which took George Borrow (1803-81) to Portugal in November 1835. The seaman's dream and its aftermath are dramatically recorded by Borrow at the start of his autobiographical work, *The Bible in Spain*. He writes:

On the morning of the 11th the sea was very rough,

and a remarkable circumstance occurred. I was on the forecastle, discoursing with two of the sailors; one of them, who had but just left his hammock, said: "I have had a strange dream, which I do not much like; for," continued he, pointing up to the mast, "I dreamed that I fell into the sea from the cross-trees." He was heard to say this by several of the crew besides myself. A moment after, the captain, perceiving that the squall was increasing, ordered the topsails to be taken in, whereupon the man, with several others, instantly ran aloft; the yard was in the act of being hauled down, when a sudden gust of wind whirled it round with violence, and a man was struck down from the cross-trees into the sea, which was working like yeast below. In a short time he emerged; I saw his head on the crest of a billow, and instantly recognised in the unfortunate man the sailor who, a few moments before, had related his dream. I shall never forget the look of agony he cast whilst the steamer hurled past him.

The ship's forward motion was stopped as quickly as possible, but not before it left the young sailor a considerable distance astern, and the ensuing rescue attempt was hampered because the vessel's single lifeboat lacked a rudder and had only two oars, which meant the seamen who manned it made agonisingly slow progress through the turbulent sea. Yet the sailor who had fallen overboard did manage to stay afloat until the lifeboat came within ten yards of him, but then he suddenly sank beneath the waves and was lost.

'The poor fellow who perished in this singular manner,' adds Burrows poignantly, 'was a fine young man of twenty-seven, the only son of a widowed mother; he was the best sailor on board, and was beloved by all who were acquainted with him.'

However, although both dreams seem to have resulted from the two men concerned directly viewing while asleep their immediate future and the accidents which killed them, it might be objected that they were simply visualising anxieties common to workers in their occupations. Coal mining and sailing were very hazardous jobs in the nineteenth century, yet those employed in them, through daily exposure to the risks involved, usually tempered or overcame their fears, just as people in dangerous jobs do today. In fact the dreams were troubling to the men precisely because they were so unusual and unexpected. This suggests that, rather than being coincidental anxiety dreams, they were indeed produced by an expansion of their sleeping consciousness, which allowed them to see the tragedy that was about to overtake them.

Equally hauntingly, the American writer Cotton Mather (1663-1728), who is best known for his torrid descriptions of alleged witchcraft at Salem, Massachusetts, records a similar preview of death by drowning in his *Ecclesiastical History of New England*. The tragic nocturnal display affected a neighbour of his, a doctor, who despite having such a forewarning in his sleep was unable to prevent the unfortunate accident from occurring. Indeed, the inability of the dreamer to stop what is shown to him from happening not only testifies to the 'direct viewing' nature of the experience, but suggests that our tomorrows have already happened and that our lives, at least where the major events in them are concerned, are following a prescribed pathway. Mather writes:

> A physician, who sojourned within a furlong of my house, for three nights together, was miserably disturbed with dreams of his being drown'd; on the third of these nights his dreams were so troublesome, that he was cast into extreme sweats, by struggling under the imaginary waters: with the sweats yet upon him, he came down from his chamber, telling the people of the family what it was that had so discomposed him. Immediately there came in two friends; that asked him to go a little way with them, in a boat, upon the water: he was, at first, afraid of gratifying them in it, but being very calm weather, he recollected himself, why should I mind my dreams, or distrust divine providence? He went with them, and before night, by a thunder storm suddenly coming up,

they were all three drown'd.

And yet 'dream previews' do not by any means feature only death and unpleasant accidents. Other occurrences, which may or may not be distressing, are likewise witnessed, although it is often those which are dramatic in nature, or of some importance or significance to the dreamer, that are seen and remembered.

For example, when I lived in Montreal in the 1970s, a Mrs M. W. of Lakeside, Quebec, wrote to me describing how one night she had the following unsettling dream:

'I dreamt someone was trying to get into my home through my bedroom window. Being unsuccessful they went to the front door and I saw them using a piece of plastic to force open the lock. I woke up covered in perspiration.'

In fact Mrs W. was so startled and upset by the strange dream that she telephoned her sister the following morning to tell her about it 'in case anything happens because she is the type who always laughs at my dreams,' although she did not, as she might have done, alert the police. But then, after having spent most of the next day out of the house, she was even more startled and upset upon 'arriving home at 4.30 p.m. to find that my home had been broken into and robbed.' Her dream had in fact shown her a preview of exactly what disquieting event was going to happen to her.

Actress Gemma Craven had a precognitive dream of a far happier nature in 1985 and which featured the man she was to marry, David Beamish.

Gemma said that one night she dreamed she was out skiing, which she has never learned to do, and that she tumbled over in the snow. Suddenly a man's hand reached down to help her up, which belonged to an unknown man dressed in a suit.

Two weeks later, she met up with some girl friends at a London hotel, who told her they were waiting for a man to join them for tea. When he arrived, Gemma immediately recognised him as the fellow in her dream, wearing the same suit, and that, as he walked over to shake hands with her, she likewise recalled the hand he held out to her. His surprise appearance rendered Gemma speechless with astonishment for the first time in her life. Their attraction to each other was immediate, and she and David went on to date and eventually to marry.

The unusual thing about Miss Craven's dream is that it interweaves fact with fiction. She remembered David, the hand he extended to her and the suit he was wearing, from the dream when she met him when awake. That part of the dream was certainly precognitive. However, their real meeting did not take place on a ski slope, but in a hotel restaurant.

This intermingling of fantasy with waking reality, which quite often happens in such dreams, is hard to understand, although the fact that the dream occurred two weeks before their actual meeting may mean that it happened on the border between what can be seen clearly and what cannot, beyond which point symbols tend to predominate. We might also postulate that the snow, the skiing and Miss Craven's fall symbolised how she then felt about the state of her emotional life, from whose coldness and loneliness she was about to be plucked by her meeting with David Beamish..

But none the less a precognitive dream may still be strangely different from the waking event when it is either expressed in symbolic terms or when the person who dreamed it acts to change the suggested outcome, even when that occurs soon afterwards. An example of the second happened to me one morning when my Great Pyrenees dog was alive, and I made the following short note of the dream I had about her:

'I dreamed that I saw my dog pick up some food she had found in the street. The food was covered with ants and they ran about in her mouth and over her tongue.'

What made this dream so fascinating is that when I took my dog out for a walk in the morning, we had not walked far when she stopped in mid-stride to smell at something, and glancing down I saw that she was sniffing at some vomit -- and the vomit was covered with ants. My dream instantly came back to me and I hurriedly pulled her head away from the vomit before she could start eating it (which I knew from past experience, she would have done). No ants therefore, or at least as far as I could tell, got into her mouth.

Yet because virtually everything in the dream matches the waking scenario, with the exception of the final outcome, the dream was precognitive. The different ending, however, suggests that 'the future' may not be entirely set in aspic and that what is previewed in dreams can be changed in waking life, when the scenario is encountered, if the dreamer reacts quickly enough to what he or she sees.

But none the less a precognitive dream may still be strangely different from the waking event even when the latter occurs soon afterwards.

Another example from my own life is a case in point. One night I dreamed that the singer Elton John (of whom I had never been a fan or had ever dreamed about before) was involved in some fraudulent scheme which involved the building of an upright, chimney-like tunnel, about six to eight feet tall and rectangular in cross-section, and which started about two feet above the ground. The idea was that Elton John would climb up the tunnel to gain access to the place where he would get the money, but as the tunnel ended in the air, it was difficult to understand how any 'fraudulent scheme' could be accomplished. Moreover, before Elton could commit the crime he was arrested and was later sentenced to three years and three days in prison.

Two days afterwards I had to fly to Athens, where I booked into an hotel on Omonia Square, a choice made entirely at the recommendation of a fellow passenger on the flight. In the bathroom of the room I was given I found there was a window with mottled glass, which I later opened, expecting it to give a view outside, to the rear of the building. But in fact it opened into a rectangular shaft running up between the floors of the hotel, and as the only light entering it came from my bathroom, I looked up and down it into blackness, so that the section visible was about the same length as the upright tunnel of my dream.

It then occurred to me that in Canada, where I had been living for the previous ten years, a bathroom is normally referred to as a 'john' -- and that 'Elton' is an almost exact anagram of 'hotel' (the letters n and h differ only by the short upward extension of the latter). The significance of my room number then became apparent: it was 303, which in the dream had been represented by the three years and three days' term of imprisonment meted out to Elton John. My dream had therefore somehow shown me in a curiously roundabout and symbolic way my discovery of that strange rectangular shaft running up beside my hotel bathroom, although I never discovered what the background motivation of fraud in the dream signified. I certainly thought the hotel bill was very reasonable.

Another Quebec woman who wrote to me about the precognitive dream she had had concerning the death of her mother noted that distance is no barrier either to the ability of the consciousness to view remote events. The lady said: 'In my dream my mother was hospitalized, had an operation, suffered very much and died. It happened exactly the same way in real life. This frightened me very much as I lived 800 miles away at the time and I didn't know of her illness until after the operation.'

Dreams that take us back into the past are less frequent than those which portray future outcomes, although this may be more apparent than real. In such dreams we may encounter people clad in old-fashioned clothing or see scenes where horses are being ridden and other animals driven along, which suggest yesteryear rather than today. Such dreams are seldom of a dramatic nature but may display some oddity of life as it once was for the people of the time. The following dream of mine is an example of this, although the actual date of my brief entry into yesteryear is impossible to determine.

My dream visit to the past took place one night in 2011. I was part of a small group of about six men, none of whom I knew, who were all clad, as I was, in formal modern day attire consisting of sports jackets and trousers, shirts and ties, socks and shoes. Then suddenly, we found ourselves, quite unsurprised and rather like a party of tourists, amongst a large audience of people dressed in eighteenth century costume and seated outside around a gentle declivity in the ground, which formed a natural auditorium, into whose 'past present' we had somehow arrived.

We manifested in an aisle of the somewhat darkened area, down which we walked and began looking for somewhere to sit. The seats there being used were chairs, stools and cushions of the period, which must have been brought out for those attending, and upon which each party of friends and/or relatives sat, gathered as they were in somewhat uneven clusters separated from their neighbours by a gap of two or three feet, through which people could pass to speak with those they knew in other groups. In addition to those informal, chance passageways, there was also the main aisle in which we found ourselves and which led down towards a flat rectangular area of roughly the size of a basketball court, bounded by a low panel wall four feet in height. This central 'stage' formed the focus of the gathering, whose members were arranged around it, and thus each seated person was facing towards it.

The audience, which consisted of both men and women and numbering, I suppose, about two or three hundred, were dressed in clothes belonging to the early years of the eighteenth century, with the women wearing long, wide, colourful dresses, which seemed voluminous, especially as they were gathered at the waist, so that their upper be-sleeved bodies, with visible bare necks and upper chests, and gloves and hats, seemed to arise from an inflated puff of material, and sparkled with the glints of necklaces, ear-rings and brooches. The men wore wigs, elegant frock coats, pantaloons reaching to below the knee, and stockings and shoes.

Moreover, because the ground on which their chairs and other seats stood was gently banked, the people sitting further back were raised somewhat above those in front of them, thereby enabling everybody to get an unobstructed view of the rectangle, which was illuminated by flares, where some display or other was evidently arranged.

We modern intruders had apparently arrived just before that performance, as the auditorium was virtually full and most people were seated, although they were still talking together, eating various fruits like oranges, pears and apples, and looking around them. Two of my group then spotted some unoccupied seats and the rest of us followed them along that row to reach them, which led to us becoming somewhat separated from one another as the spare seats occurred singly or in pairs between different audience groupings, who fortunately did not seem to mind us sitting ourselves down upon them, and who, in fact, did not take any notice of us at all, which was odd because we were dressed so differently from themselves.

Our attention was then summoned by the blast of a trumpet from the rectangle, and I saw a man, who had stepped forward at one end, blowing the instrument. Almost immediately a group of about twenty young men, lightly yet romantically clad in Elizabethan tights of various colours, loose shirts and shoes, and holding rapiers, pushed passed him into the rectangle, while from the other end entered a second body of similarly dressed and armed youths, who, after standing and surveying each other for a short while, then began advancing towards one another, not in a straight line but with those at the centre leading the way. When the leading men met they began fencing with each other, their foils clashing, which stimulated the watching audience to begin cheering and calling out words of encouragement.

I watched this strange 'Elizabethan' martial contest with surprise and puzzlement. I realised that the men within the rectangle were not real Elizabethans who had somehow dropped into what would be for them a 'future present' to fight one another, but rather were eighteenth-century youths wearing Elizabethan costumes, although I had no idea what was happening because there had been no prior announcement about it and there was no dialogue between the combatants to reveal what was going on.

The audience, however, obviously did know, which was why they were assembled there and had been waiting for the show to start. Their expectation of seeing people in different costumes helped explain, I thought, why they paid so little attention to us 'moderns' arriving amongst them, especially as the colours and cut of our clothes were muted and modest in comparison with their own and those of the performers.

The fight in the rectangle now became more general and seemingly more serious. Those towards the rear of each group came forward and began fencing with their opposite numbers, whereupon the shouting became louder and more boisterous, and amid the mêlée blood was shed. A man towards the front suffered a sword thrust and blood appeared immediately on his shirt, which increased when he staggered and took another thrust and then suddenly dropped to the ground. I could hardly believe what I was seeing. Then another was wounded but gallantly fought on, raising shouts of approbation from the audience, until he too received another rapier thrust, bled profusely, and then also collapsed.

From then on the bloodletting increased as more and more men were wounded, some seemingly receiving rapier thrusts right through their bodies, which sent them immediately to the ground. I could hardly bear to watch such carnage, which had already brought me to my feet, and before I knew what I was doing I found myself running down the aisle towards the rectangle to make some sort of protest, although I hardly knew what, against such ghastly bloodletting. I could not understand how the participants in the fight were prepared to be wounded or killed to provide a show for others, who were cheering them on with such abandonment. It made no sense at all.

My arrival at the boundary of the rectangle brought me much closer to the action, however, and I soon saw that the fight was not real, despite appearances. The rapiers were all blunted, and the blood was red dye which came from small sacs hidden under the shirt of each combatant, on the front of their chests, and which could be broken to release their contents if prodded with a blunted rapier. Thrusts seemingly through the body had passed harmlessly between chests and arms, and the excitement of the audience came from a suspension of belief on witnessing the fighting and on hearing the shouting of the participants, rather than from any reality. And the costumed young actors did put on a good if grim show, with plenty of fencing, parrying and thrusting, whilst they bled, collapsed and died with a will.

It was initially horrible to watch yet once one knew it was theatrical pretence, one could savour the blood and the death without feeling guilty about it or at all shocked, which I suppose was the whole point of the spectacle. Professional wrestling, which has a similar capacity to rouse an audience, is, I suppose, the nearest modern equivalent to what I witnessed in the dream.

It was at that point that I woke up and so left the 'past present' of nearly three hundred years ago behind. I therefore had no chance of seeing how the entertainment of that evening ended or of finding out who my 'modern' companions were, or of talking to any of those who lived then. I had been too distracted and overawed by the spectacle provided by the audience and by the drama which then occurred on the rectangular stage to do so. It was, none the less, a wonderful experience and indeed the sheer number of people dressed in eighteenth century fashions gathered together in that outdoor theatrical arena, where we 'moderns' joined them to watch forty youths clad in Elizabethan costumes fighting with rapiers, suggests that I had somehow managed to project not just my consciousness but my whole self down my time line into that 'past present' rather than creating a dream fantasy with no foundation in fact.

I have no idea if such entertainments were held in the early eighteenth century, or even later, but if they were, they would have been quite easy and inexpensive to set up. It was, after all, an age when men still carried swords, and many young men enjoyed fencing and practised the art regularly; and if the aristocrat (as I presume him to have been) who organised the display on his estate had provided the fighting group with Elizabethan costumes, which could be borrowed or hired, he really only needed to get his grounds-men to erect a low rectangular fence around a natural, flat, dry declivity on his land to make a suitable site for the mock contest to take place. And if the participants were the sons of some of those in the audience, they would both have gained an added thrill and pleasure from their performance.

As similar excursion into the past in a dream was described by Peter Ackroyd in an article published in *The*

Times in August 1996. The dream not only took him back to the eighteenth century but into a particular year of the nineteenth too, and he was able to direct his consciousness into both past-presents, whereas my visits were chosen for me by my sleeping mind.

Ackroyd revealed that on the night in question, when he was asleep, he had a dream in which he realised that he was dreaming, which very seldom occurs, whereupon he quickly said to himself, 'I want to be taken to the eighteenth century.' His command to himself was instantly obeyed and without any sense of movement or hesitation, he suddenly found himself outside walking along a darkened roadway, with buildings on one side of it, and passing pedestrians who were clad in eighteenth century clothes.

In fact he could not help but notice that the houses he passed and the clothes of the people in the street were all noticeably redolent of the style of the early eighteenth century, and seemed, in this regard, to be entirely authentic.

He also had the wherewithal, unlike myself, to speak with one of those walkers and to ask him where he was. He was told that he was in Hendon, which today is a busy suburb in north-west London but which was then a small village in the county of Middlesex.

'I asked to be taken to the pest-house or hospital – at which point someone laughed, and said that they were the same thing'. Just then Ackroyd suddenly saw the pest-house in front of him; he went into it, but found the odour there so strong and repugnant that it caused him to retch and to quickly dash out. It was then that his dream of that time ended.

This last detail, however, sounds unlikely because small villages in the early eighteenth century, like those today, did not have hospitals. Sick people were nursed at home by their parents or spouses, and if an apothecary or doctor was required, who might live in another village, he would have to be sent for. The apothecary would prescribe whatever medicine he thought was needed, which would probably have been an herbal remedy.

But while Peter Ackroyd's dream visit to Hendon came

thereby to a sudden conclusion, he did not wake up but found himself back in the earlier dream state that led to it, in which he was climbing some stairs, whereupon he said to himself, 'I wish to be taken to 1858'.

As soon as he spoke, a door appeared in front of him, which he opened and, passing through it, found himself inside a large house whose decor, carpeting and fittings were recognisably mid-Victorian. He then went through a door on the landing which brought him into a study with the same Victorian ambience, and there he was quite soon joined by a woman, who was not only dressed in a costume of the period, but who appeared to know him very well and to be expecting him, although not, it seems, quite so early. He tried to explain his precipitate arrival by saying that he had needed some air and that, before he realised whither he had wandered, he was there with her. He then asked her to describe where the house they were in was situated, and she obligingly told him that it stood in West London, or more specifically, in Kensington.

He next left the house and found himself, to his bewilderment, in a street that was recognisably mid-19th century in style, the doors bearing letter-boxes and knockers, the buildings fronted by spiked railings, and the street illuminated by gas-burning lamp-posts; although the dream terminated suddenly when, to his further astonishment, 'a late-20th-century London taxi pulled up' !

Peter Ackroyd's two dream sequences are made more surprising by the fact that he had some control over where he went, which is rarely attained, although this awareness naturally introduces a conscious directorial element into what then happened, allowing his mind do what was asked of it by perhaps creating two scenes one after the other that seemed to him entirely real. Indeed, they were so lifelike that he feared that he might not be able to get away from them.

I also sensed this possibility of becoming entrapped when I first arrived amid that large group of people, yet their apparent unawareness of me and my unknown 'modern' companions suggested that they could not perceive us, and that we were, in that respect, rather like ghosts from 'the future' amongst them.

CHAPTER THREE

INTO THE FUTURE

Where art thou, beloved Tomorrow?
When young and old, and strong and weak,
Rich and poor, through joy and sorrow,
Thy sweet smiles we ever seek, --
In thy place – ah! well-a-day!
We find the thing we fled -- Today.

Tomorrow by Percy Bysshe Shelley

The 'previews' of future events described in the last chapter which take place in dreams, can also happen when we are awake, although they do so infrequently. One of the most interesting of them was described by J. B. Priestley in his famous book *Man and Time*. A correspondent had told him how, when she was a maid at Dunraven Castle in South Wales, she one day found herself in the kitchen with the senior-maid, Renate, and the odd-job boy, Hans:

She next said that she saw Renate pick up a jug containing some chocolate sauce and then turn to give it to Hans, but that as she did so she dropped it on the floor, where it smashed. Its contents spread out to form an irregular, amoeba-like pattern on the floor. But then, to her horror, the scene melted away and then started again. This caused her to shout at Renate, as she picked up the jug, not to touch it, and to scream in terror as the scene repeated itself, the jug smashing again and producing the same seemingly predestined irregular shape of the chocolate sauce on the floor.

But although the maid quickly told the distressed Renate why she had screamed at having seen the scene repeat itself, both Renate and Hans angrily retorted that if she had not screamed, the jug would not have been dropped!

This suggests that if our consciousness can occasionally extend itself to give us an accurate view of events lying in what we call 'the future', it implies that consciousness is travelling along what is, in effect, a pre-ordained pathway, one formed by each of our individual lives, and that we therefore have little or no control over what happens to us.

If so, we really are ruled by what the ancients called fate or destiny, whether we like it or not. Such a scenario is certainly suggested by those dream 'previews' mentioned earlier which deal with the dreamer's own death, as those concerned were unable to prevent what happened to them, despite having seen what was to be, although when the tragedy happened to someone else, the dreamer, by being made aware of the danger, was sometimes able to forestall it. And dreams which display trivial happenings can lead to preventative changes being easily made in waking life.

Waking 'previews' can take someone much further into 'the future'. And such time-slips are by no means limited to passive viewing, as they frequently involve the apparent merging of two presents, so that a 'future present' becomes part of the observer's present, while sometimes the person concerned, like the objects described in the second chapter, is wholly introduced into another time, thereby becoming, in science fiction parlance, 'a time traveller'.

Wolfgang Goethe (1749-1832), the German poet, once met himself while out for a ride. This is how he described the incident:

> I was riding on the footpath towards Drusenheim, and there one of the strangest presentiments occurred to me. I saw myself coming to meet myself on the same road on horseback, but in clothes such as I had never worn. They were light grey mixed with gold. As soon as I had aroused myself from the day dream the vision disappeared. Strange, however, it is that eight years later I found myself on the identical spot, intending to visit Frederika once more, and in the same clothes which I had seen in my vision, and which I now wore, not from choice, but by accident.

The phenomenon of the double or doppelganger is a well-attested and intriguing one, which I considered thoroughly in *Doubles: The Enigma of the Second Self*, and while there are many accounts on record of people seeing their own doubles, it is none the less rare for anyone to encounter their double in the guise of themselves in the future, as happened to Goethe. In fact the poet's experience is so unusual that rather than being a straightforward separation, it appears instead to be a time-slip brought about by him seeing directly through, as it were, the invisible barrier separating himself from the 'future present' in which he simultaneously existed, to thereby bring about a merging of the two. For clearly, it he had viewed the future by expanding (or moving) his consciousness along the 'time line' of his life, then he would have seen his surroundings through the eyes of his older self.

In the early eighteenth century Martin Martin investigated instances of what is traditionally called second sight among the inhabitants of his native Skye and the other Hebridean islands, which he included in his book about the Western Isles. He noted that the Seers, as he called such psychically gifted individuals, often saw a scene of, say, a marriage or a funeral, as it actually would occur at some future date. Hence they had essentially the same experience as Goethe, except that they saw other people instead of themselves. The Seers would often, for example, perceive a traveller who was shortly to visit their community, dressed in the clothes worn on the day of his (or her) arrival, and be thereby apprised of his coming. A church minister named Daniel Morison was thus descried some days before landing on the island of Rona:

> Upon my Landing (said Mr Morison) the Natives receiv'd me with their usual Salutation to a Stranger, 'God save you, Pilgrim, you are heartily welcome here; for we have had repeated Apparitions of your Person among us, after the manner of the second Sight; And we heartily congratulate your Arrival in this our remote Country'

Martin noted the Seers normally had previews of future events that involved members of their own families or their neighbours' families, or of strangers who visited them, and not of activities taking place in the outside world. This again indicates that they were then seeing through the invisible barrier separating them from the future event.

Martin writes: 'I have been seen thus myself by Seers of both sexes; some that saw me in this manner, had never seen me personally, and it happened according to their visions, without any previous design of mine to go to those places, my coming there being purely accidental.'

Those islanders without the gift of second sight would also sometimes be shown the future in the same way. Martin records that when several Harris men were sailing around Skye bound for the Scottish mainland, they suddenly saw, much to their astonishment, a dreadful vision of two men hanging by the neck from the mast of their ship. They realised the phenomenon was caused by second sight, yet they had no idea what it referred to or why it should have happened. Martin writes:

> They pursued their voyage, but the wind turn'd contrary, and so forced them into Broadford in the Isle of Skie (sic), where they found Sir Donald MacDonald keeping Sheriff's Court, and two Criminals receiving sentence of death there, the Ropes and Mast of that very boat were made use of to hang those Criminals. This was told me by several, who had this Instance from the Boat's Crew.

The men were therefore able to witness a notable future event some days before it actually happened, although as I explained earlier what they saw was there and then taking place in the timeless Oneness (as indeed it still is).

Canadian folklorist Helen Creighton investigated second sight among the descendants of Scottish settlers in, appropriately, Nova Scotia, and she 'was amazed to find this strange faculty possessed by so many people'. Of particular interest is her observation that most of the sightings of future events witnessed by such psychically gifted immigrants did not involve incorporeal or ghost-like figures, but rather solid, three-dimensional people who would, if necessary, move them aside to pass by. Such an amazing viewing was. and perhaps still is, by no means uncommon, and she mentions the names of several men who had been pushed out of the way by people following a funeral that was yet to occur, and who could identify the horses used during it.

These astonishing examples suggest that in addition to 'looking ahead' by gaining a view through the invisible divide that separates the seer from a future event, some can effectively negate that divide and thus bring together the present inhabited by the seer with the 'future present' in which the event is occurring. And such time-slip intermingling of 'the present' with either 'the past' or 'the future' can on occasions happen, as the Harris islanders discovered, to ordinary people, either singly or in groups.

For example, at around 8.30 in the evening of 31 May 1859, the Reverend Spencer Nairne took a stroll along the main street of Aberdeen arm-in-arm with a cousin-in-law named John Chalmers. They had arrived by steamer from Edinburgh some four and a half hours earlier, accompanied by several other family members and friends, and all were scheduled to leave the city together when the steamer sailed at 9.30 p.m., bound for Thurso. Both men were enjoying their walk, which was a postprandial one, along the busy and still sunlit street. But then, recorded the Reverend Nairne, something very odd happened.

> While we were walking and talking there passed me, going in the opposite direction, a lady whom I recognised named Miss Wallis . . . She was walking with a gentleman, holding his arm and talking with some animation, and I saw plainly that in the moment of passing she had seen me and recognised me. I at once dropped my friend's arm and turned round to speak to her, quite expecting that she would do the same by me. Not only, however, had she not done so, but so far as I could see, she had completely disappeared. I looked everywhere, up and down the footpath and across the road, walked quickly on in the

direction she was going, and then turned back again, but not a sign of her could I see. I also looked into a good many of the shops in the immediate neighbourhood and satisfied myself that she had not turned into any of them.

The disappearance of Miss Wallis and her gentleman friend was not supernatural, in the sense that they were both at one moment walking along the main street of Aberdeen but then suddenly vanished. And neither did the Reverend Nairne, as perhaps might be thought, encounter doubles of the two people concerned; nor was he mistaken in whom he thought he saw. Indeed, the answer to what he experienced is more bizarre than any of these possibilities, and was revealed when he met up with Miss Wallis, whom he had known since childhood, about four months later in London. To his surprise, the lady upbraided him for 'cutting' her in Aberdeen, saying that she had passed him in the street while walking with her brother but that when she immediately turned to speak to him, neither he nor his companion was anywhere to be seen. Astonished, the Reverend Nairne hurriedly told Miss Wallis about his trip to Thurso, from whence he had gone to Norway, where he had stayed for about three months, from 6 June to 8 September.

> 'Well,' she said, 'but when were you in Aberdeen?'
> 'On May 31st.'
> 'But,' she objected, 'I was not in Aberdeen then. I spent a week there with my brother in the latter part of July. I have recorded my meeting with you in my journal and if I had the book here with me I could show you the entry. I have never been in Aberdeen before or since.'

Hence remarkably, there was an interval of almost two months between the day on which the Reverend Nairne and his friend took a stroll in Aberdeen and the one on which Miss Wallis and her brother took theirs. Miss Wallis also said that she and her brother had walked through Aberdeen and had passed the Reverend Nairne and his friend earlier in the day; the encounter did not take place, she insisted, in the evening.

If the details and the dates are as the Reverend Nairne gives them, then two seemingly different and widely separated moments came briefly together and merged as if they were one. But of course they were and are one: after all, Mr Nairne was quite conscious of being in 'the present' when he took his walk, just as Miss Wallis was when she took hers. This is why we cannot say that the whole episode happened because Spencer Nairne and his friend were momentarily transported into 'the future', or because Miss Wallis and her brother were momentarily taken back into 'the past'.

Rather, both couples were (and still are!) part of the same eternal present, yet occupying two 'separate' loci within it, and the Reverend Nairne and Miss Wallis were somehow able to simultaneously 'peer through' the invisible divide between them and so descry each other. How that happened is presently unknown, although it may have been triggered by the fact that Mr Nairne and Miss Wallis knew each other another well and were psychically connected.

One of the most famous and dramatic examples of a 'forward' time-slip happened to Air Marshall Sir Victor Goddard (1897-1987), a highly reputable witness, in 1935, as he flew a Hawker Hart biplane from Turnhouse air base, near Glasgow, Scotland, where he had gone to play golf, back to Andover, Hampshire, where he was stationed. He was blown off course by a bad storm shortly after take-off, when he suddenly spotted a row of hangars beneath the low black clouds. He recognised them as part of the derelict and unused First World War airport at Drem, which he had coincidentally visited the day before. He headed towards the airport, intending to take fresh directions from it, but when he flew over the perimeter fence, the whole vista beneath him changed.

He wrote that the airfield was bathed in bright sunshine and that it appeared to be fully operational again. He noted the rebuilt hangars, the order of the scene beneath him and the new-mown grass, and the presence of four aeroplanes on the tarmac, namely three Avro 504 biplanes and a monoplane, which he could not identify. Two mechanics were pushing a second monoplane of the same type out through the open doors of one of the hangars. The aircraft were all painted in a brilliant yellow chrome, and, equally unusually, the two mechanics and their colleagues elsewhere were all wearing blue dungarees.

As Goddard knew, there were no yellow aeroplanes then in service, and neither were there any monoplanes. And RAF mechanics still wore their standard brown overalls, not the blue dungarees he had seen. But what particularly surprised him was that none of the mechanics so much as glanced up as he flew by in his noisy aeroplane about 30 feet above them; indeed, it seemed as if they were somehow completely unaware of both him and his machine.

It took Sir Victor Goddard no more than twenty seconds to fly right over the four hangars of the renewed airport, but then, upon passing over the last hangar, he suddenly found himself back among dark storm clouds and the driving rain. Yet he was able, none the less, to make the necessary course correction, and he flew the Hawker Hart aeroplane on to reach Andover safely. When he recounted his remarkable experience to his Wing Commander, who knew, as did everybody else, that Drem airport was an abandoned ruin, he was jocularly advised to cut down on his drinking!

But four years later, in 1939, with war looming on the horizon, Drem airport was rebuilt and repaired and turned into a RAF flying school, whose training aircraft, several of which were Magister monoplanes (these did not exist in 1935), were all painted yellow, the new designated colour (it had previously been silver). And during the intervening period the colour of RAF mechanics' uniforms was changed from brown to blue.

Sir Victor Goddard's experience is sometimes described as a 'vision', one that allowed him to look into the future. Yet it seems clear that he actually had a spontaneous and completely unexpected time-slip, in which a 'future present' was somehow intruded into 'the present' of which he and his plane were a part. And despite him suddenly flying into sunlight and over a newly built Drem, there were no other indications that anything amazing had happened. His aircraft continued to handle entirely normally, yet it was not a complete part of the future scene, because its passage overhead went unobserved by those on the ground. Hence despite Goddard's awareness of his own and his aircraft's solidity, as well as the airport he flew over, both he and his plane could not apparently be seen or heard by those below.

But there was one feature of the repaired airport seen by Sir Victor which did not match the 'real' thing. This was the hangars, which Sir Victor noticed were rebuilt in brick, although they were actually later reconstructed in steel. Bricks had been used to build the original hangars, and it was initially decided to rebuild them with bricks (of which Sir Victor knew nothing, for the decision to rebuild the airport was not taken until after his experience). However, before the work on the airport began the plans were revised and steel was chosen instead of bricks. This curious difference suggests, as I shall discuss in more detail in the next chapter, that there may be more than one reality or dimension of being, and that in one of them new brick-built hangars were erected at Drem. If so, it was over this Drem airport that Sir Victor flew, not the one that was eventually constructed in our 'reality'.

Another sudden and unexpected coming together of the present and the future, which was also recorded by Helen Creighton, happened to two sisters living at Bridgeville in Pictou County, Nova Scotia, during the early years of the twentieth century.

Miss Creighton records that the girls were woken one night by the sound of a train, which caused both of them to scramble out of bed and go to the window, from where they saw a train passing by in the mid-distance. This astonished them, as they had never seen a train before and knew that there was no railway track for one to travel along. However. during the next year land surveyors came and work soon began on a railway track, which in due course was used by trains following the route which the girls had previously descried.

This time-slip incident gains credibility from the fact that 'the future' landscape was witnessed by two young women at the same time, which suggests that it was objective, not subjective. We may therefore perhaps conclude that for some unexplained reason 'the future' landscape, with a railway track and a train, intruded itself into, or became merged with, the landscape as it then was, so letting the sisters preview what, from their point of view, was to be.

Martin Martin records that such views of future landscapes were common among the Seers of the Scottish islands.

He writes:

> It is ordinary with them to see Houses, Gardens and Trees, in Places void of all three; and this in process of time used to be accomplished, as at Mogshot in the Isle of Skie, where there were but a few sorry Cowhouses thatched with Straw, yet in a few years after, the Vision which appear'd often was accomplished by the building of several good Houses on the very spot represented to the Seers, and by the Planting of Orchards there.

The cases mentioned above demonstrate that when a time-slip happens the future scene becomes instantly and unspectacularly a part of the present. There are no intermediate stages or dramatic accompanying effects, or indeed anything initially to warn those who view it that such a wonderful merging of two moments has occurred.

Such time-slipping smoothness was certainly a feature of the time-slip undergone by a boy who grew up to be a senior academician, whom Joan Forman in her description of his experience identifies as Professor H., and which took place at Hanley, in North Staffordshire, in 1896, when he was seven years old. The remarkable event had several unique features which make it particularly interesting. The first of these was the prior appearance of a doorway in a previously blank end wall of a street, on the other side of which lay an expanse of open, uncultivated ground. The strange doorway was noticed by young H. when he played truant from school one afternoon, and the temptation it offered proved irresistible.

He said that when he went through the door he suddenly found himself in an unknown small town, where the houses all seemed to be devoid of human life. He entered one of them and climbed up the stairs to a large room. The window gave him a view to the east out over the surrounding but unrecognisable countryside. The land sloped down to a valley, beyond which were a range of tree-covered hills.

At that moment the 'vision', as Professor H. calls it, ended and he found himself back in the street, staring with some surprise at the now doorway-less wall, wondering what on earth had happened to him. He had, however, no further insight into his puzzling experience until nearly twenty-one years later, when he fought at the Somme. There, following many months of static trench warfare, the Germans, early in 1917, made a surprise tactical retreat of some forty miles, which gave the British forces an opportunity to enter and reconnoitre the deserted area, an operation in which Professor H. took part.

During the advance he came to a deserted village named Misery, where he found himself, much to his surprise, in the street of his earlier vision, except that several of the houses contained dead Germans. One of them was empty of corpses, however, and on climbing the stairs he came to the same large room, facing east, whose window overlooked the same landscape, although the Somme river was out of view.

Hence as a seven-year-old boy Professor H. had evidently entered, with one important exception, the same village that he did in 1917, and so was wholly taken 'forward' in time. But as with Victor Goddard and his sighting of the restructured Drem airport, the village he walked through did not fully accord with the 'real' one, for he failed to encounter any dead Germans, who were very much in evidence in 1917. This may either mean that the young Professor H. visited Misery after the corpses had been removed, or that he happened luckily to miss entering those houses that contained them. The other possibility is that, like Goddard, he witnessed a variant of 'the future', which, if so, further suggests that 'the future' is not wholly confined to one unvarying path, but has several, or perhaps even many, branch lines.

The above-mentioned cases taken together indicate that time-slips involving encounters with 'the future' can occur in four principal ways, although none is entirely self-contained:

a) A Future Encounter of the First Kind happens when the consciousness of a person moves or expands 'forwards' along the 'time line' of his or her life to directly view a particular future event in it.

b) A Future Encounter of the Second Kind occurs when a person is somehow able to 'look through' the invisible divide between his or her present and a 'future present'.

c) A Future Encounter of the Third Kind involves an apparent merging of a portion of a 'future present' with the observer's present, so that the former comes to occupy an area around him much like an enclosing bubble.

d) A Future Encounter of the Fourth Kind happens when a person is wholly introduced into a 'future present', so that he or she in effect becomes a part of it. This may also involve a change in geographical position, as happened with the young Professor H., although there is no sense of physical movement.

Time-slips into the past can also be divided into four similar kinds, although Past Encounters of the Third Kind and of the Fourth Kind happen more frequently than do their future equivalents. Yet time-slips of the Fourth Kind, which do not happen spontaneously, are particularly difficult to accomplish and maintain.

The doorway seen by Professor H. as a boy, which appeared in a brick wall at the end of a street, has a parallel in the opening lines of Leonard Clark's 1948 poem *Encounter*:

> *A mist fell,*
> *And without warning a door swung open;*
> *I stood naked between mountains.*

The poem's ending mirrors Goethe's meeting with himself in the future:

> *A figure in the terrible distance moved towards me*

As relentless as day advances upon night,
Nearer it came and slower I
Went out to meet it.

It was myself.

I have not been able to determine if Clark's poem was based
on an actual experience of his, but I suspect that it might
have been. People become poets because they have a
sensitivity beyond the ordinary, which puts them in touch
with the hidden spirit-forms of nature and with the Oneness
that lies behind the apparent linear progression of everyday
life. This is why no great poem is composed; it is received as a
gift.

Alfred, Lord Tennyson (1809-1892), a former poet-
laureate, was not only blessed with unusual perceptivity but
could easily attain a trance state, wherein he had direct
experience of God. He once apparently underwent a time-slip
of the second type listed above, when he saw the aerial
combat characteristic of the Second World War, which lay
nearly a century in 'the future', and he wrote a description of
the event in his poem *Locksley Hall*, published in 1847. I
believe the reader will agree that it is an astonishing preview:

'For I dipt into the future, far as human eye could
see,
Saw the Vision of the world, and all the wonder that
would be;
Saw the heavens fill with commerce, argosies of
magic sails,
Pilots of the purple twilight, dropping down with
costly bales;
Heard the heavens fill with shouting, and there
rain'd a ghastly dew
From the nations' airy navies grappling in the
central blue;
Far along the world-wide whisper of the south-wind
rushing warm,
With the standards of the people plunging thro' the
thunder storm;
Till the war-drum throbb'd no longer, and the battle-

flags were furl'd
In the Parliament of man, the Federation of the
world.'

The concept of reincarnation maintains that the liberated soul-form of a deceased person is transferred, either immediately or after an interval, which may be long or short, into the about-to-be-born body of someone else, who is usually unrelated to him or her, which means that for all of us our present life is the latest in a succession of lives. The memories of those former lives stay with us, although they cannot normally be recalled.

Yet through past life hypnotic regression some people have been able to remember who they once were and what sort of lives they led. Indeed, serious research into reincarnation conducted by academics like the late Professor Ian Stevenson have found cases of physical and emotional similarity between those claiming to be the recipients of such soul-form descent, which is impossible to explain in any other way.

But what is even more interesting, and of direct relevance to the subject of this chapter, is that some people have undergone the opposite process, which may be called 'future life hypnotic progression', and have thereby been made aware of lives in their time-line that lie in 'the future'. If their accounts are fact rather than fancy, it provides further evidence that 'the future' exists alongside, so to speak, 'the present', as it likewise does with 'the past'.

It is impossible, for obvious reasons, to prove if such recovered 'memories' of future lives are real or if they are elaborate fantasies. But none the less the notion is intriguing. And when such a person as Jenny Cockell, who has had the recollection of one of her previous lives startlingly verified, recounts that she has recalled, through hypnosis, several future existences, the notion may be more than hot air.

Jenny Cockell, assisted by hypnotist James Alexander, investigated four of her future lives. The first happens during the first half of the 21st century, when she becomes a Nepalese peasant woman named Nadia. The second, and somewhat imprecisely recalled life, is spent as a Polish woman, and dates to around the year 2150. After that, she becomes an American biochemist called Janice Thorpe, who resides in the early twenty-third century, and then, later that same century, she manifests as another American woman named Sheryl Vaughn, who seems to be some sort of student. The future, as seen through the eyes of the last two, is a bright and generally peaceful place, yet has suffered massive depopulation, apparently caused by twentieth- and early twenty-first century chemical pollution, which has negatively affected human fertility. The oceans, Ms Cockell maintains, are polluted, although the air is clean.

Because her views of the future are seen, as I mentioned above, through the eyes of her future physical selves, as were those of her past lives by her former selves, it means that the 'time line' of her present life does not start at her birth and end at her death, but instead passes through all her lives, so that they are connected together (as are ours) rather like beads on a thread. Hence her sightings of the future are not 'future memories', but rather are time-slips brought about by the movement of her consciousness along this invisible 'line'. They are, in other words, Future Encounters of the First Kind.

Jenny Cockell's coming life as Nadia is the most fully visualised, and indeed her descriptions of the Nepal countryside, its people and their way of life, buildings, and religion, seem to quite closely match those of present-day Nepal, which presumably will not be all that different in twenty or so years' time. However, the reality of Jenny Cockell's remarkable journey into that future life will not be known until a Nepalese woman named Nadia is discovered in c. 2040, and who, when under hypnosis, recalls that she was Jenny Cockell in her previous existence.

CHAPTER FOUR

ENCOUNTERS WITH YESTERDAY

There was a Door to which I found no key:
There was a Veil past which I could not see:

From the *Rubáiyát of Omar Khayam* trans. by Edward FitzGerald

Those writers of science fiction who have their characters travelling through time usually portray them as doing this by riding aboard some advanced technological device, like that envisioned by H.G. Wells's eponymous *The Time Machine* or the Tardis of television's *Dr Who*. But as we have seen, the nature of time is quite different from how these writers imagine it to be, and indeed the builder of a time machine would be disappointed to find there is no past and no future, as he or she understands them, for his or her product to travel into.

Indeed, we have already discovered, contrary to the evidence of our senses, that time manifests as an undifferentiated or Eternal Oneness, a timeless everlastingness, which contains within itself both the birth of the universe and its end, and everything in between. Its seeming division into a past that has already happened and a future that is yet to come is a product of the limited field of view of our individual consciousness, for when our consciousness is widened, as it is, for example, during a state of enlightenment or mystical awareness, a very different picture emerges.

The German mystic Meister Eckhart (*c.* 1260-1328) once had a revelation about what we call time, of which he wrote:

> In eternity there is no yesterday nor any tomorrow but only Now, as it was a thousand years ago and as it will be a thousand years hence, and is at this moment, and as it will be after death . . . The Now wherein God

made the world is as near this time as the now I am speaking in this moment, and the last day is as near this Now as was yesterday.

The same curious perception of timelessness was experienced by the Swedish polymath and psychic Emanuel Swedenborg, who writes in *Heaven and Hell*, his book about the next world, that 'although all things in heaven have their successions and progressions as in the world, still the angels have no notion or idea of time and space, and so completely destitute are they of such an idea that they do not even know what time and space are.'

In fact mystics and contemplatives throughout the ages have discovered that the multiplicity of material forms we see and the linear progression of time we experience are illusory, and that reality, as I have said, consists of a unity or Oneness, containing within itself nothing that is separate or distinct. Thus we are all intimately connected with everything around us, to the extent that we are as much a part of each other as we are of ourselves; and indeed, it is neither impious nor improper to claim that not only do we exist in God or the One, but that we are as much a part of Him as He is Himself.

This is why time travel cannot take place in the way that H. G. Wells and other authors have imagined it, and neither is it travelling in the sense that they mean it. For the distant past, to paraphrase Eckhart, is no further from us than yesterday, and the distant future no further from us than tomorrow; rather, the whole of history and of futurity exist with us now, at this moment, and if we could but broaden our field of view we could gaze out across a plain filled with browsing dinosaurs as easily as we could watch whatever creatures will be at the centre stage of life 100 million years in 'the future'. We do not at present know how to bring this about, but such interaction can certainly happen spontaneously when the moment is somehow right for it to do so.

Johann Heinrich Zschokke (1771-1848), whose unusual surname is pronounced *Tchok'keh,* a German writer of histories of Bavaria and Switzerland and also of many fictional works, acquired when a young man a particular talent, which he called his 'inward sight', whereby he was occasionally able to view incidents which had occurred to someone who was previously unknown to him. He explains in his autobiography:

> It has happened to me sometimes on my first meeting with strangers, as I listened silently to their discourse, that their former life, with many trifling circumstances therewith connected, or frequently some particular scene in that life has passed quite involuntarily, and as it were dream-like, yet perfectly distinct before me.
>
> I would relate to those whose life had passed before me the subject of my vision, that I might thereby obtain confirmation or refutation of it. It was invariably ratified, not without consternation on their part. I felt a secret shudder when my auditors replied that it was true, or when their astonishment betrayed my accuracy before they spoke.

Zschokke's remarkable ability, while sporadic in its manifestation, is an example of a Past Encounter of the Second Kind, for he was able, while watching and listening to an unknown man or woman, to see in graphic detail in his visions some past event or other of his or her life.

'For a long time I held such visions as delusions of the fancy,' he elaborated, 'and the more so as they showed me even the dress and motions of the actors, rooms, furniture, and other accessories.'

But this is what we would expect him to see if he was gazing directly into the usually very ordinary 'past-present' moments or episodes of a stranger's life.

He describes in some detail what was once revealed to him about a young man who had sat opposite him in the Vine inn at Waldshut, where he had gone with two companions to dine after a long walk, and who was expressing his opinions about the Swiss with a candour that was indiscreet.

'This man's former life was at that moment presented to my mind,' said Zschokke. 'I turned to him and asked whether he would answer me candidly if I related to him some of the most secret passages of his life, I knowing as little of him personally as he did of me.'

On getting the youth's assent Zschokke described what he had seen, 'and the whole company were made acquainted with the private history of the young merchant; his school years, his youthful errors, and lastly with a fault committed in reference to the strong box of his principal.

> I described to him the uninhabited room with whitened walls, where, to the right of the brown door, on a table, stood a black money box. A dead silence prevailed during the whole narration, which I alone occasionally interrupted by enquiring whether I spoke the truth? The startled young man confirmed every particular, and even, what I had scarcely expected, the last mentioned.

It may be suggested that Heinrich Zschokke's ability to have Past Encounters of the Second Kind was brought about by telepathy, which allowed him to 'read' the minds of those concerned, yet if so, we would not expect it to have been so occasionally demonstrated, so dominated by the visual, and the images so replete with minor details. He did not think or feel what he related, he saw it. He looked right into the lives of those occasional strangers whose past was revealed to him in such detail and diversity, and which remains so astonishing and enigmatic to this day. Indeed, Zschokke himself met with only one other person who possessed a like power. He was an elderly peripatetic seller of oranges and lemons, from the Tyrol. 'He seemed, nevertheless, to value himself somewhat upon this mysterious wisdom,' comments Zschokke, unlike himself, who regarded it as a talent of no use whatsoever.

Sightings of the past by hindsight happen less frequently than do those of the future by foresight. Yet where direct viewing is concerned, whereby a 'past present' becomes merged with the present of the observer, as happened with Zschokke, the opposite is true. There is also more 'whole body' merging with the past than there is with the future, although because 'the future' lies hidden behind a glass, darkly, this may be more apparent than real.

William Ward, a commercial traveller for Caley's chocolate company, which was based in Norwich, had a surprise encounter with a dramatic past event in the early 1930s, and my maternal grandfather Herbert Cole, with whom he was friends, wrote an account of it in his popular weekly column which appeared in a county newspaper. The incident in question took place one November night when Billy, as he was familiarly called, slept in 'a fine bedroom attached to but outside' the Talbot hotel, a hostelry located in a small Gloucestershire town..

'It was the first time I had visited Gloucestershire,' Billy Ward said. 'I knew no one in the locality and had no associations whatever with the place I had to visit. My instructions were to visit the little town of --- to pick up the threads of some dropped business.'
(The unnamed town was possibly Cirencester, wherein still exists an ancient Talbot Inn.)

After Billy had dined, he spent an hour or two talking and smoking (but not drinking, as he was then a staunch teetotaller) with some of the other guests. At about half-past ten, feeling very tired, he decided to turn in for the night. The hotel proprietor showed him to his somewhat unusual bedroom, which was the only one available in the otherwise fully booked hotel.

> He lighted a lantern as we emerged from the hotel, and we walked a few yards to the left until we came to a flight of stone steps, up which we clambered. He unlocked a huge oak door and we entered a big oak-beamed room. To me it seemed to be an old tithe barn on to which the more modern hotel was built. The oak beams and the roof were black with age, the floor was of black oak with rugs here and there, the windows were tall and narrow. At the further end was a huge four-poster canopied bed, and its side was parallel with the long side of the room, so that if I sat up in bed I could survey the whole room.
> '

Having thanked his host and bidden him good night, Billy Ward quickly undressed and climbed into the ancient and imposing bed, which he was pleasantly surprised to find was very comfortable. He blew out the candle and soon fell asleep.

> The next I knew was that a terrific bang had awakened me, and I sat up with a jerk, my heart pounding wildly. There was a bright moon, and though it was not shining directly into the room there was sufficient light to see things quite distinctly. I remember glancing at my watch and noting the time, half past one.

To his astonishment and fright, Billy then heard some whispering from the room's far end, opposite the door, which came, he noted with growing alarm, from a group of indistinct and seemingly tense figures huddled together there. Then he heard footsteps outside, along with a murmur of voices and the clink of metal. He noticed that the figures became completely silent as those outside, whoever they were, reached the building, which revealed that they were hiding from them.

> Suddenly a violent attack was made on the door. An axe was evidently being used. Louder and louder and faster and faster came the blows. I could hear the splintering of wood and the laboured breathing of the men who were striving to break in. As the door grew weaker under the assault and groaned on its hinges some of the shadowy figures at the further end of the room came forward and clustered quietly around it; and I could then see, as they were nearer to me, that they were all in helmets and breastplates, with swords and pikes in their hands. Some were richly dressed, and their hair hung in curls upon their shoulders.
> 'Crash! went one of the door boards, and a face was poked in through the aperture. One of the men inside the room made a vicious thrust at it with a pike. There was a scream and the face disappeared, followed by a storm of shouting and a redoubled

attack on the door. All at once it gave way and fell inwards with a crash, and in poured several men, pushed forward by those behind. The broken door had now let in more light and I could see clearly that the attackers were similarly armed to those in the room, though of rougher appearance.

The fight was now fully on and I was intensely interested. I was no longer afraid, but instead I felt exactly as if I was watching a "talkie". It was a glorious scrap. Backwards and forwards the parties swayed, and as the defenders were pushed back more and more men entered the room, until perhaps thirty or forty had crowded inside the door. The room was filled with shouts and groans, curses and invocations to the Deity, clash of steel upon steel, and thud of steel upon skulls. I saw one man's skull split to the chin with an axe. Dead men lay here and there and the wounded crept to the side of the room. One person I noticed particularly. He was tall and slight, richly dressed, with curling hair and a pale face. He took no part in the fight; in fact, I do not think he had even a sword in his hand. He remained at the further end of the room and in front of him was a ring of the tallest men of the party, who fought like fury whenever the attack pressed in their direction.

And so the fight went on. Now the invaders were driven to the door; then with a rush the defenders were pushed to the other end of the room. The numbers of effective men on both sides were rapidly growing less, when all at once a shrill whistle blew. The invaders backed to the door, leaped down the steps, and disappeared.

That was the full extent of the incident, which ended as rapidly as it had begun, and Billy Ward was aware of nothing else until he suddenly awoke the following morning 'at half-past seven feeling like a wet rag'. His memory of the bizarre episode came flooding back, astonishing and disturbing him, yet he could only think by way of explanation that he must have had a particularly vivid dream. He told the landlord about it when he went in to breakfast. The man, however, was not unduly surprised by what he heard. When I had finished, he said:

> You are not the first who has had that experience. But
> let me tell you, you have dreamt nothing. You have
> reconstructed something which actually happened in
> that very room between Cavaliers and Roundheads in
> the Civil War. I wish that I could see it, but I can't,
> though I have slept in that room many times. The
> story you have told me, however, is identical with
> what others who have slept there have told me.
>
> The facts are these. In the Civil War, Gloucester
> City alone stopped the Cavaliers' route of
> communication between Bristol and the North. It was
> so much a thorn in the scheme of their operations
> that the King himself came down to urge his army to
> take the city, and he made this town his headquarters.
> It was his room and his bed that you occupied.
> Gloucester was in a bad plight and on the point of
> surrender when the Earl of Essex came to its aid, and
> he made the first stroke to relieve it by clearing the
> Royalists out of this place. It is extremely probable
> that it was only a small party who knew of the enemy
> quartered here. Perhaps it was only chance which led
> to the attack, for it is certain that they never knew or
> guessed that the man in the background was Charles
> King of England, or the result would have been
> entirely different. What you saw last night actually
> happened in August 1643, as all the records testify.

The siege of Gloucester by the royal army led by King Charles
I began on 10 August 1643, and lasted for twenty-six
gruelling days, until the city was finally relieved, as the
landlord correctly stated, by parliamentary troops
commanded by the Earl of Essex, who had marched there
from London, on 5 September 1643.

However, the incident viewed by William Ward would
almost certainly have taken place in the first week of
September, for historians relate that Charles only learned of
the approach of Essex's army on 4 September, and that he
accordingly raised the siege on the following day, when
Essex's troops were being deployed on the heights of

Presbury, about five miles from Gloucester. Essex himself entered Gloucester with his men on 8 September, bringing both timely relief and much-needed provisions to the half-starved inhabitants.

William Ward's remarkable experience was not, as we have seen, a vivid dream, and neither was it, as perhaps might be supposed, a haunting. Not only do ghosts rarely appear in groups, but by no means all of the men who were seen by Mr Ward died on the night of the attack. Hence it is extremely unlikely that they would all assemble together to re-enact what was, after all, a comparatively minor and brief encounter in a long civil war that was filled with such incidents.

Indeed, the evident solidity of the figures, the reality of the action, the sounds made, which were many and varied, and the splitting and destruction of the room's door, together suggest that Billy Ward had somehow witnessed a real, but past, event as it happened, which in turn indicates the incident was a Past Encounter of the Third Kind, whereby a night in early September 1643 was brought together with the night when Billy occupied the same room in the early 1930s. However, it is interesting to note that the fighting men do not seem to have been aware of Billy Ward, sitting astonished in his bed, and it is fascinating to wonder what might have happened if he had had the wherewithal to step out of it and tap somebody on the shoulder.

A very similar account of how a person staying at an old inn saw an event which had previously taken place in the room he occupied, so that he was effectively there when it happened, is related by Helen Creighton. The incident occurred in the early 1830s, and the man who had the strange and unnerving experience was a young army officer stationed at Annapolis Royal, Nova Scotia.

After taking a room at the inn there and retiring to bed, the officer fell asleep quickly but was later woken by someone trying to get in through the door, which he had closed and bolted. But none the less, he suddenly found that two uniformed officers were in the room, dressed in tricorn

Robert Devereux, 3rd Earl of Essex

hats and long turned-down topboots, who appeared to be, as he later recalled, 'very gallant gentlemen'. Without .uttering a word to the startled man in bed or to each other, both removed their military coats, drew their swords and began fencing, a combat that went on until one ran the other through and killed him. He then, to the dumbfounded watcher's horror, picked up the body and threw it out of the window. He then left the room somehow and so ended the strange and unsettling incident.

While it is unfortunate that nothing was said by the men to indicate their nationality, Miss Creighton remarks that because their uniforms were either seventeenth or eighteenth century in style, they would almost certainly have either been from France or England, as troops from both countries were garrisoned at Annapolis Royal during that period. The event was wholly real and disturbing to the watching young soldier: and, of course, it was real if a time-slip had somehow merged his present with the 'past-present' of the duellers, even though they, like the soldiers seen fighting by Billy Ward at the Talbot hotel in Gloucestershire, were entirely unaware of his trembling presence in the nearby bed.

This lack of awareness is a feature of many, but by no means all Past Encounters of the Third Kind. Yet when the person concerned remains invisible to those whom he sees, he may be detected by their animals, notably by their dogs, which naturally suggests that when a dog whines and raises its hackles in response to a seemingly invisible presence, it may be reacting not to the visiting spirit-form or ghost of a dead person but rather to someone who has entered our present from either 'the past' or 'the future'. Some ghosts may even be the result of a Past Encounter of the Second Kind, the person who sees them 'looking through' the invisible divide that separates his present from theirs.

Canine awareness was a notable feature of the time-slip experienced by Laura Jean Daniels, a resident of the American town of Dearborn, Michigan. On the night in question, Laura Jean told journalist Joyce Hagelthorn, who wrote up her remarkable story in the *Dearborn Press* in May, 1973, that having worked very late at her office, she decided to walk home through the deserted streets. There was a large moon in the sky, and as Laura Jean neared her apartment, the clouds parted to reveal its full brightness, causing her to stop and gaze up at it. But when she lowered her eyes, she found herself, to her complete astonishment, in a different reality. For without any warning, the town that she had been walking through had disappeared.

She saw that the houses bordering the street had gone and that the sidewalk along which she was walking had become a brick path. The air was now redolent with the smell of honeysuckle and roses. Some way ahead she saw a thatched cottage and as she came nearer to it she noticed that a man and a young woman, who wore 'very old-fashioned clothes' were seated together in its garden, fondly embracing one another.

Yet when Laura Jean reached the gate of the cottage, on which she put her hand, a small dog suddenly ran towards her from underneath a nearby bush and began to bark at her. The animal was trembling, and when the man looked up and called to him to desist and asked him what he was barking at, Laura realised that the man could not see her, even though she could feel the touch of the gate and smell the odour of the flowers. Then while she was trying to decide what to do, she glanced back behind her and there saw her street, with its houses and other modern features. And when she turned back towards the cottage, she found that it was no longer there. She saw instead that she was in the middle of her own city block, a short way from where she lived. The cottage, the brick path, the couple and the dog had all disappeared.

Because the entire town of Dearborn in which Laura Daniels lived had previously vanished, it seems that she had undergone a Past Encounter of the Fourth Kind, which took her wholly back into the landscape of a 'past present', one that perhaps had formerly occupied the very spot where she had been walking in 1973. She was able to perceive the pleasant rural scene (which perhaps dated from two hundred years before) and the two lovers, and could smell the scents, hear sounds, and both touch and feel the cottage gate through which she was about to pass. Yet although she was sensed, and reacted to, by the small dog, she evidently was not visible to its owner. Hence in this regard she herself was like a ghost.

This was not the case with a young English woman who experienced two remarkable time-slips in the 1970s. I shall call her Elizabeth to preserve her anonymity, and she lives in Malvern, Worcestershire. The first time-slip took her 'back' several hundred years and brought her face-to-face with a youth who was badly frightened by her unexpected manifestation. The incident happened one evening after Elizabeth, who had put her children to bed and was alone in her living room, her husband being then away working in London, was sitting by the fire reading a book. She said:

> What sort of book it was I can't remember, but suddenly I hit upon a perfectly ordinary paragraph which acted as a sort of catalyst. There was an abrupt jerk as if I had been catapulted out of my chair and then, to my surprise, I was standing in a round room made of bare stones with a slit of an unglazed window

63

opening on to trees. Trees, restless trees without number, tossing their dark green tops with a sound like the sea, and birds, birds singing their hearts out. I was staggered by the sheer volume of sound and then I glanced across the room –- a distance of no more than eight feet –- to a kind of a bench on the opposite wall and, sitting up with terror in every line of his face, was a young man, staring at me as if I was a demon straight out of Hell.

Elizabeth divulged that on that evening she had been dressed completely in black, wearing as she was a black polo-neck jersey, black trousers, and black boots, and that her long red hair hung down well below her shoulders. She was also made-up with lipstick and heavy eye-shadow.

He must have thought I was a bona-fide black and scarlet devil such as he had been warned about and there was no time to reassure him that I was harmless. Poor young boy! Even now I feel guilty.

I have no idea why that innocuous paragraph acted as a trigger but I know that, for a split second, I had been in the medieval world and had terrorised the poor innocent lad who quite clearly saw me.

And while Elizabeth would still like to apologise to the boy for scaring him so badly with her sudden and completely unexpected entry into his life, brief though it had been, she remains equally startled by the volume of sound that she heard in the woodland outside the house where she saw him.

'Now, whenever I hear or read,' she added musingly, 'of the supposed silence of the ancient forests, I can think if only you knew. Lord, the noise!'

Elizabeth's time-slip is distinguished from many others by its brevity and by the fact it was seemingly brought about by her reading an unremarkable passage in a book which prompted her to experience 'an abrupt jerk as if I had been catapulted out of my chair' and which introduced her into the 'past-present' of the boy, and which was, thereby, a momentary Past Encounter of the Fourth Kind for her.

But contrarily, those who experience a time-slip and become both visible to, and can interact with, the inhabitants of a 'past present' sometimes discover, much to their surprise, that the solidity of the latter is not quite as tangible as it appears.

This was a feature of the Past Encounter of the Third Kind that happened to three men, the driver of a post chaise and his two passengers, who were journeying together through the Gloucestershire countryside one Christmas Eve in the 1820s. The time-slip was seemingly prompted by the driver stopping his vehicle at a cross-roads, and found he was uncertain of the road to take. Just then he noticed a large house standing nearby that was gaily lit up for the Christmas season, and on bringing it to the attention of his passengers, the older of the pair, who wanted nothing more than to stretch his legs, volunteered to walk there and enquire which road led where. This he did, and the door of the house was opened by a servant, yet before the traveller could question him about the road they should take, the house's owner emerged from the dining room, from which also came the sound of happy talk and laughter, and invited him to step inside and participate in the celebrations. He would, the man insisted, be made very welcome.

The traveller thanked him but politely refused the unexpected invitation, saying that both he and his companion were eager to get to their destination before Christmas Day, and they only wanted to know which road to take to get there. The owner smiled regretfully, wished him the compliments of the season, and kindly instructed another of his servants to walk with him to the cross-roads and to show the post chaise driver the right road. When the servant had done that and was about to return to the house, the grateful traveller took a coin from his pocket and dropped it into the palm of the man. Yet to his absolute astonishment and horror, the coin fell through the man's outstretched hand to the ground, at which moment he disappeared, as did the house from which he had come.

The incident was so curious and disturbing, that the two travellers made enquiries about the house and its occupants during the following days, and were startled to learn that the only house built close to the cross-roads had been demolished some thirty years earlier, following a dreadful murder which had been committed there one Christmas Eve. This suggests of course that the murder happened on the very Christmas Eve that the 'time travellers' intruded upon, and that the coming together of the two presents was somehow initiated by the energies (for want of a better word) still present there.

Another enigmatic Past Encounter of the Third Kind involving a house took place one afternoon in 1946 as Bruce MacMahon and his sister Grace walked around the edge of Great Wood near Hadleigh, in Essex (which was then a much more rural area than it is today). To their surprise the pair suddenly came across a large and impressive Georgian mansion standing in a clearing in the wood. They had never seen it before, despite having walked through and around the wood on many previous occasions. As they stared at it dumbfoundedly, wondering how they could have missed it, they saw a young woman dressed in up-to-date clothes and accompanied by an Alsatian dog walk down the drive, and they watched her until she disappeared over the brow of a nearby hill. Then they shrugged their shoulders bemusedly and continued on their way.

But when they later returned back the same way, the brother and sister were amazed to find that the mysterious mansion and the clearing in which it had stood were no longer there. Both had seemingly vanished into thin air. The perplexed MacMahons even returned several times to the wood to search for the house, but without success; and equally puzzlingly, none of the old maps of the area showed such a house, and neither did any of the local historical records make reference to it. Hence Great Wood, as far as they could determine, did not contain, and never had contained, the Georgian mansion they had seen.

If the brother and sister both saw what they said they did, it is evident that the mansion and the clearing it stood in had temporarily entered their present. But where had it come from? It obviously wasn't a part of 'the past' that was recorded in the old maps and other documents the MacMahons examined. It might have come from 'the future', where mock Georgian mansions will perhaps at some date be fashionable, but if so, how can we explain the girl wearing 1940s clothes?

The other alternative is bizarre but it is none the less worth mentioning, because it seemingly explains the apparent anomalies: the mansion did come from 'the past' but not from 'our past'. It came instead from the past of another reality or time channel that parallels our own but which is separate from it. There may in fact be several, many, or even an infinite number of different dimensions of being that coexist alongside our own and partially or wholly mirror it. These will of course contain replicate versions of you and me and everyone else, and they thereby allow each of us to simultaneously explore other possibilities and directions. A man or woman who is, for example, a homeless person here, might be a monarch in one of those other realities, and vice versa.

We had a previous indication of this strange state of affairs in the brick-built hangars seen at 'the future' Drem airport by Sir Victor Goddard, and in the village without dead Germans walked through by Professor H as a boy. Similarly, we may perhaps suppose that there is an alternate time channel wherein a Georgian mansion was erected in Great Wood, which still exists in their 'today', and it was that house along with two of its 'present' occupants (the girl and her dog) who made an appearance in our Great Wood in 1946. If so, we can only hope that the girl and her canine friend managed to get back to the house in time to 'return' to their dimension with it.

And it is not only human beings and their houses that can enter our present from 'the past'; old natural landscape features can also do the same. In her autobiography entitled *The Joy of the Snow*, author Elizabeth Goudge recounts the experience of a friend of hers who suddenly and without warning found herself in a beautiful wood as she motored home across a part of Dartmoor:

She drove through the wood without realising that she

had never done so before, as she was aware only of the beauty of the trees and the moonlight filtering through them. When she eventually came out of the wood, she found that she had reached her cottage, where she parked the vehicle and went inside. It was only later that she remembered that her route home should have taken her through a stretch of open moor, not a wood. The next day she told an aged male acquaintance, who had lived all his life on the moor, what she had experienced. He said that he knew of the wood and that he had once seen it himself, but added that she would never see it again, that it was, in effect, a once in a lifetime experience.

The next case I shall discuss has much in common with the scene witnessed at the Talbot hotel by William Ward, most notably in that it has been experienced by different people at different times and because it features a brief and otherwise unimportant incident in the life of someone who, like King Charles I, was a tyrant, and who played a strangely significant role in British history. However, unlike King Charles, whose violent and untimely death was touchingly described by the poet Andrew Marvell . . .

> He nothing common did or mean
> Upon that memorable scene,
> But with his keener eye
> The axe's edge did try;
> Nor call'd the gods with vulgar spite
> To vindicate his helpless right;
> But bow'd his comely head
> Down, as upon a bed.

. . . the man was a foreigner and a usurper, and he is scarcely remembered today.

His full name was Marcus Aurelius Valerius Carausius, a Roman citizen born in the Low Countries, and he came to prominence in AD 285 when he was made admiral of the Roman fleet -- the *classis Britannica* -- based in Gesoriacum (modern Boulogne) and was given the job of clearing the Channel of pirates. This he did with considerable success, but when it was found that he only attacked the pirates after they had raided the mainland, which gave him the opportunity of seizing their plunder for himself, he was condemned to death (in AD 287) by the emperor Maximian. This prompted the wealthy, headstrong, violent and suddenly fearful Carausius to sail his large and powerful fleet to Britain, where he declared himself its supreme ruler or Augustus. And remarkably, he governed Britain as a rogue, yet independent state for the next six years, until he was murdered by his accountant in AD 293, thereby demonstrating that with a strong navy these islands could successfully resist continental control (in this case by the Roman empire).

During those heady six years of independence Carausius constructed a number of defensive forts on the English coast, of which two were built in East Anglia. One was at Branodunum (modern Brancaster), on the north coast of Norfolk close to the Wash, the other at Gariannonum (modern Burgh Castle), on the east coast beside Breydon Water, in north Suffolk.

One of the rivers that meanders across the Norfolk Broads to lazily discharge its waters into Breydon Water and thence into the sea is the Bure. And it was up this river, on the 21 July 1829, over fifteen hundred years after Carausius's death, that Lord Percival Durand went yachting with four male friends. The aristocratic party sailed as far as Wroxham Broad, where they anchored, went ashore, and then walked across to the 120-acre expanse of fresh and glistening water. Finding a large tree conveniently placed beside it, they sat in its welcome shade, talking together and admiring the view. But none of the young men were at all prepared for what happened next, for without any warning an old and very ugly man, dressed in what appeared to be ancient Roman costume, suddenly stepped in front of them and glared at them in an angry, questioning manner.

He was an uncanny looking person (wrote Lord Durand to his father) whom one might reasonably suppose to live in a hole in the ground . . . a forbidding-looking person indeed. His mouth was very large, and the lower jaw had dropped somewhat, revealing some ragged and discoloured teeth, several of which were missing. No one saw him arrive, and no one saw exactly what eventually became of him when he left us.

The visitor sternly demanded to know what they were doing there, and told them that they were trespassing on Crown land. When Durand, puzzled, asked him what exactly he meant by that, the man told him, to their astonishment, that the surrounding *jugera* (or, loosely, acres) were the property of Caesar. Hearing this but stifling their smiles, the young tourists enquired which particular Caesar he was talking about, and their interrogator informed them with a frown that it was Marcus Aurelius Carausius, Emperor of Britain.

This convinced Percival Durand and his friends that the man was a lunatic, but none the less they all resolved to humour him. They asked him his name, and discovered that it was, or so he said, Flavius Mantus, and that he was the Custos Rotulorum, or Keeper of the Rolls, for the whole of eastern Britain.

> 'But tell me, Flavius,' demanded Lord Durand, winking at the others, 'why are you here today? The Roman Empire relinquished these islands fifteen hundred years ago.'
>
> 'You are right, and you are wrong,' the man replied without hesitation. 'the 20th Legion of Auxillaries of the Belgae left here as you say, but the Roman Empire in the West never relinquished these islands. The Empire continues here today as of old, and I am still the Custos here . . . and it is our noble Emperor's birthday!'

He then turned and gestured grandly towards Wroxham Broad, and added that a great celebratory festival was soon to take place in the stadium. He even asked them if they could see Carausius' banner floating over the royal box! This absurd question was sufficient to remove any lingering doubts which the Englishmen may have had that the ugly man in fancy dress was completely insane, yet it did not stop their eyes turning to gaze in the direction that he pointed.

What happened next left them breathless with astonishment. Lord Durand continued:

The waters of the Broad had rolled back and transformed themselves into a huge stone wall enclosing a most sumptuous Roman amphitheatre with terraced seats all around, and thousands of silken banners and bannerets were fluttering in the breeze from the copings. The arena was turfed with a velvet sward of surpassing beauty, and thousands of people in Roman costume were flocking from all directions and passing in to their seats. Already there were bands of soldiers in Roman armour strolling about, and several chariots with prancing white chargers were moving around to the far side of this huge Hippodrome. We rubbed our eyes and pinched ourselves to try and convince ourselves that we were not dreaming, but it was all genuine enough, and everybody was in a happy mood and the noise of this excited concourse floated up towards us.

Then Flavius Mantus excitedly shouted: 'Today our great Emperor arrives by road from Branudonum, on his return with his fleet from Gessoriacum, and here he comes!' Yet on looking around at him, the five incredulous Englishmen found that the ugly old man had somehow become transformed into a young Roman officer clad in a handsome uniform, who was seemingly a younger version of himself. Loud hurrahs rose from the amphitheatre and trumpets sounded, and, turning towards the noise, the young men saw a magnificent procession enter the gaily decorated enclosure:

Then a mighty roar of welcome went up, as a large golden chariot drawn by ten white horses in sumptuous harnesses came in. Around the chariot were twelve full-grown lions led on golden chains by warriors in gilt armour carrying glistening halberds. The cavalcade made a complete detour of the arena whilst the golden chariot bearing the Roman general took up its position in the centre.

'See!' exclaimed the Custos, swelling with pride. 'There is the greatest man this country has ever known. There stands before you the great General Marcus Aurelius Valerius Carausius, Count of the Saxon Shore, Primicerius Notariorum, Emperor of the Most Noble and Honourable Roman Empire of the West. From Branudunum in the East to Portus Adurni in the South, from Isca in the South-West to Camelon in the North his name is the greatest in all Britannia. See, now he descends from his chariot and leads the way to the royal box . . .'

The man continued extolling the feats of the new Emperor, notably his latest success in repulsing some raiding bands of Danes and Jutes, against whom he had put to sea with his fleet and had decisively defeated them in a great sea battle, and whose surviving warriors were now the prisoners Carausius was bringing with him into the arena. And as the Englishmen watched, those very men fell to their knees before the Emperor and began begging his forgiveness for their criminal actions.

'Then slowly,' added Durand, 'the entire apparition faded out from our view, and in a moment the span of water resumed its normal appearance, and the Roman officer had changed back to the old man once more, and, wandering away amidst the trees, disappeared.'

This astonishing time-slip is a Past Encounter of the Third Kind, in which a portion of the 'past present' containing the Roman amphitheatre entered the present inhabited by Lord Durand and his friends like a bubble. It is made even more compelling by the fact that the four Englishmen witnessed it together, which would seem to assure its objectivity, and on a summer's day, which prevents it from being dismissed as a dream. Hence like Willam Ward, they saw a comparatively unimportant, but none the less dramatic, historical event -- not as it happened centuries before -- but as it is still happening.

The Wroxham Broad time-slip has affected other people, yet interestingly their experience of it has not taken place in exactly the same way. For example, in 1603, a local man named Benjamin Curtiss was swimming across the Broad 'from the Bure-side to that opposite' with two friends, when their feet, despite the water at that point being about fourteen feet deep, suddenly and unexpectedly touched the bottom, and . . .

> (We) presently found ourselves, recounted Curtiss, standing in the middle of a large arena with much seats one above the other all around us. The water was gone and we were standing there dressed as Roman officers . . . What is more astonishing still, we were not surprised neither were we incommoded by this piece of enchantment, but rather were we quite accustomed to it, so that we forget that we had been bathing. (Spelling modernised)

The three men then watched the entrance into the amphitheatre of a long and magnificent Roman procession, which was so like that seen by Lord Durand and his friends, including the pathetic lines of prisoners chained together, that it would seem to be the same. And not long afterwards, as happened with Lord Durand's party, the remarkable and noisy scene faded and disappeared, as did the trio's acquired Roman costumes, and they again found themselves splashing about in the cold lake.

But while their apparent 'whole body' entry into the Roman amphitheatre suggests that they had a Past Encounter of the Fourth Kind, how can we explain their sudden transformation into Roman officers? This is very puzzling, yet I believe it can be elucidated, as can the time-slip itself, by assuming that the three men had been those Romans in a previous life, and that their consciousnesses slipped 'back' down the 'time line' connecting them together, so enabling them to once more see Carausius' magnificent birthday celebrations. If so, this means that they really had a deep Past Encounter of the First Kind. And presumably it was their coincidental presence at the same spot together in 1603 that somehow 'flicked' their consciousnesses back into the heads of their former selves. This would also perhaps explain why Curtiss remarks, 'We were not surprised neither incommoded by this piece of enchantment'.

Equally surprisingly, and like Lord Durand and his

friends, a church parson named Thomas Penston with a couple of companions, in the spring of 1709, sat down on the bank of Wroxham Broad to enjoy a picnic, when they were, wrote the Reverend Penston,

> Suddenly and very peremptorily ordered away by a very undesirable looking person whose appearance and clothes belied his refinements of natural good breeding. As we were somewhat enangered by this unpleasant person's persistence, we made to go away, when suddenly we had to quickly stand aside to make passage for a long procession of regal splendour, the outstanding characters of which were a golden chariot containing a hideous-looking man dressed as a Roman general, and drawn by ten white prancing stallions, about a dozen lions led in chains by stalwart Roman soldiers, a band of trumpeters making a great noise, and another band of drummers, followed by several hundreds of long-haired, partly armoured sea-faring men, or sea-soldiers, all chained together.

However, despite the Reverend Thomas Penston and his friends initially meeting up with, or so it seems, Flavius Mantus, the Custos Rotulorum, the lake did not similarly vanish to reveal an arena, as happened with Durand's party, but instead those in the procession mysteriously disappeared when they reached the edge of the Broad. And neither were they noticed by anyone in the procession. Yet none the less, this occurrence was, like Durand's, a Past Encounter of the Third Kind.

It may be objected by the sceptical that the two parties who encountered Flavius Mantus were improbably able to communicate with him in English, whereas if the Custos had really been a man of the third century AD he could not possibly have understood or spoken our language, which did not evolve from that of the Angles or Engle until several centuries later.

Lord Durand remarks of him: 'His voice I would say was cultured in tone, but there was something about his diction that was not quite English.'

We must then remember that Flavius Mantus first manifested into what was for him a 'future present' to chide the people on the banks of the Broad before they saw the scene in the Roman amphitheatre. This suggests that he is not confined to that 'past present' of his, but rather is able somehow to step out of it and visit other 'future presents'. And if he can do that he will presumably have had plenty of opportunity to learn English.

Flavius Mantus also intriguingly told Lord Durand's party that, 'the Empire continues here today as of old, and I am still the Custos here.' But what can he have meant by that? Well, because the Oneness contains within itself the whole span of what we call history, the Roman Empire, and every other empire for that matter, continue to exist in 'past presents' that are coincident with, and as real as, the present we seemingly occupy. We are in that regard surrounded by Romans and ancient Celtic tribesmen, who flit through our world like shadows, unseen and unheard, as we do through theirs. Flavius Mantus would have been (and still is) fully aware of this, because having discovered how to step from one present into another, he knows that nothing passes or fades away.

The time-slip undergone by Billy Ward has been experienced, as I mentioned, by several other people, yet it is not linked to a particular date in the calendar. The same is true of the one that occurs at Wroxham Broad. Sometimes, however, time-slips happen with more regularity, and may sometimes occur on the anniversary of the past event in question. One of the best examples of a regularly repeated time-slip was experienced by Bernard Hutton and members of his family, along with some friends, in the summer of 1923. Indeed, the incident as described below was not only remarkable for being witnessed by several people but also because they were able to communicate with those who had come from 'the past'. Hence they became a full part of the time-slip scene for as long as it lasted.

The incident took place on the North German island of Sylt, one of the Friesland group, where Bernard Hutton and his two sisters and brother, accompanied by a family friend named Fraulein Arnold, had been taken on holiday by their parents. They stayed in the seaside town of Westerland, where the Huttons had rented a house for the duration of their stay. Another family from Berlin, a Captain Schulhof, his wife and two daughters, were occupying a nearby villa, and it wasn't long before the Huttons and the Schulhofs met up with one another and became holiday friends. Then, a few days later, on 2 August, Mr Hutton senior left the island for Berlin, where he had some unfinished business to complete, and he was waved goodbye from the local railway station by his parents, his siblings and Fraulein Arnold, and by the Schulhofs.

On leaving the station the two family groups decided to go for a walk together along the island's beach and to return to Westerland by train from one of the outlying stations. It was a fine day for such a hike, and the sea was completely calm. The adults and children enjoyed their ramble, which took them to a number of small fishing villages, where they watched the inhabitants mending their nets and attending to other necessary maritime repairs. Yet when they reached the small local railway station in the early evening they found that they had missed the last train, which obliged them to return by foot along the coast, a distance of about four miles.

When they had walked about two miles, they suddenly came across a wide bay, in which the water was being buffeted and made very rough and dark by a strong wind, whereas the sea further out remained as calm as ever. None of the party thought this was initially strange, as their attention was taken by the sight of a small fishing boat that was in danger of being swamped by the huge waves.

They then noticed a group of men on the beach clad in oilskins attempting to launch a lifeboat. Attracted by the drama, the Huttons, Schulhofs and Fraulein Arnold ran on to the beach, where they soon descried another body of men dressed in oilskins preparing to fire a lifeline across to the fishing boat by means of a small cannon. They heard the noise of the cannon when it was fired, and saw the line hurtle out to the boat. Yet the agitated motion of the vessel and the waves crashing over her prevented the fishermen aboard from catching hold of it, and the line fell uselessly into the sea. One of the cannon-firing team then shouted: 'Get the other line ready, Erwin.'

The holidaymakers were now at the rough sea's edge, and they watched with intense interest and concern as the cannon was hurriedly charged with a second line. The cannon fired again, and they once more saw the lifeline snake across the water towards the boat. But then, to everyone's dismay, the boat was again swept by waves and the line lost. Captain Schulhof ran to the men launching the lifeboat, who were about to set off, and frantically yelled at them:

'Do you need any help? May I join you? I'm a naval man.'

To which their captain somewhat brusquely replied, 'No thanks. This is a matter for Friesians only.'

And with that they rowed away from the shore, pulling hard on the oars in a desperate effort to reach the fishing boat before it sank. The latter vessel's sad plight and the attempted rescue operation had meanwhile brought a number of women and their children to the beach, who stood watching the proceedings in a stunned and anxious silence. The cannon firers were preparing to discharge a third lifeline out to the stricken vessel, but before they could do so the fishing boat suddenly disappeared beneath the waves, bringing groans and cries of dismay from all. The cannon-firing men immediately dashed to another rowing boat, pushed it into the sea and jumped aboard, and furiously rowed out after the other. They made faster progress, and soon caught up with the first. But just then a tremendous wave crashed against both lifeboats, overturning and sinking them. Bernard Hutton's mother screamed:

'How terrible!'

As she uttered those horrified words an amazing change happened. The wind-tossed sea of the bay became suddenly still, and the Huttons and their companions, turning to look down the beach, were equally astonished to find that the men, women and children who moments earlier had been there with them had vanished, as had the cannon. There was in fact nothing to indicate that anything untoward had happened. The only object visible on the otherwise deserted shoreline was a large stone cross standing some way back from the sea. Captain Schulhof impulsively marched across to it. Moments later he called out to the others to join him. When they reached the monument, they sombrely read the inscription carved upon it:

> To the eternal memory and glory of our beloved husbands and brothers, our fathers and sons, who perished in the cruel and merciless sea, while bravely trying to rescue their comrades when their fishing vessel foundered on the evening of August 2, 1872. May God have mercy on the souls of these eighteen fishermen and the would-be rescuers and may they have eternal peace.

It was only then that Captain Schulhof's companions, who together formed a group of four adults and six children, understood they had somehow witnessed the re-enactment of an event which had occurred on the same date fifty-one years earlier. And when they reached the next village, where they made enquiries about the tragedy, they were introduced to the local priest who, much to their surprise, told them,

> It happens every year on August 2, at the same time of the disaster. Many people have seen exactly what happened in 1872. I myself have seen it twice.' To which he added: 'I had intended to go to the bay this evening to witness (it) again . . . but, unfortunately, I was detained by an unexpected visitor

He then took them to his house and showed them a leather-bound book in which previous startled onlookers had written up and signed their accounts of it. He explained that he had now discontinued this 'lengthy procedure', but he invited them none the less to add their signatures to the book, which they accordingly did.

This time-slip, by taking place in the context of an open seascape, enabled the witnesses to notice that it only involved the water of the bay, which became unaccountably rough, and its beach, while leaving the surrounding area quite unchanged. This means that the bay and the human events which had occurred there in the 'past present' of fifty-one years earlier had somehow intruded themselves into 'the present' of 2 August 1923, thereby completely overlaying or displacing the conditions in the bay as they were then. It was, in other words, a Past Encounter of the Third Kind.

The floundering fishing vessel, the two other boats, and the cannon, along with all the people taking part in the tragic event, appeared entirely solid and normal to the watching Huttons, the Schulhofs and Fraulein Arnold, who had no idea that they were witnessing something that had already happened. And they too, unlike some who have been involved in a time-slip, were seemingly quite visible to those attempting the rescue, one of whom Captain Schulhof spoke with and offered his assistance. We can only wonder what would have happened if Captain Schulhof had been taken aboard the lifeboat and given an oar to pull on. He would certainly have lost his life, but would his body have been found floating in the bay of 1923 or in that of 1872? If the latter, would it have resulted in the beach monument spontaneously changing to record the sad loss of nineteen persons?

But remarkable though that event was, the most famous example of time-slipping is that which happened to two educated, middle-aged English women, named Charlotte Anne Moberly and Eleanor Jourdain, respectively the Principal and Vice-Principal of St Hugh's Hall, an Oxford college for women, when on Saturday, 10 August 1901, they together visited the grounds of the Petit Trianon (or Small Pavilion), which lies about a mile to the north-west of the Palace of Versailles, outside Paris, France. Eleanor Jourdain returned to visit the site on her own the following January, when she had a similar encounter with 'the past'. The two women, using the pseudonyms Elizabeth Morison (Moberly) and Frances Lamont (Jourdain), wrote an account of their incredible experiences in a book entitled *An Adventure*, which was published in January 1911.

It was at about 4 p.m. on that August Saturday afternoon in 1901, when the women were at Versailles, that Charlotte

Moberly suggested to her friend and colleague that they should walk to the house and gardens called the Petit Trianon, which in 1774 had been given by King Louis XVI to his wife and Queen, Marie Antoinette. On receiving Miss Jourdain's assent, the two women followed the main avenue leading to the adjacent Grand Trianon without difficulty, but once arriving there they were uncertain how to proceed to the Petit Trianon. However Miss Jourdain, acting under impulse, took one particular path, beside which she soon saw a woman and a teenage girl standing on the steps of what looked like a farmhouse, while Miss Moberly, following after her, spotted a woman shaking a duster from the window of another house. Later Miss Jourdain wrote:

> I particularly noticed their unusual dress. Both wore white kerchiefs tucked into the bodice, and the girl's dress, though she looked thirteen or fourteen only, was down to her ankles . . . the woman was standing on the steps, bending slightly forward, holding a jug in her hand. The girl was looking up at her from below with her hands raised, but nothing in them. She might have been just going to take the jug or have just given it up. Her light-brown hair escaped from under her (close white) cap. I remember that both seemed to pause for an instant, as in a *Tableau vivant*; but we passed on, and I did not see the end.

Soon afterwards the two English women came across two men 'dressed in greyish-green coats and small three-cornered hats', whom they thought were gardeners as they had a wheelbarrow and a spade with them, and of whom they asked directions to the Petit Trianon. Taking the path indicated, both women were then overcome by a powerful feeling of loneliness and depression, when they arrived at a small wood, within which was a 'light garden kiosk, circular, and like a small bandstand' and beside which sat a dark-complexioned, pock-marked and unpleasant-looking man, who wore a black cloak and a broad-brimmed slouch hat. He turned to look at them but said nothing, and Miss Jourdain commented that his 'expression was very evil and yet unseeing, and though I did not feel that he was particularly looking at us, I felt a repugnance in going past him'.

Just then, to their surprise, another man came running up, who likewise wore a black cloak and an unusual hat with a wide brim, although he was tall and handsome, and had a very red face. The breathless newcomer, however, hurriedly showed them the right path to take, and this soon brought them to a small rustic bridge, which they crossed, and then they went through another small wood to emerge from it near the Petit Trianon, which turned out to be a 'square, solidly-built country house'. As they crossed the rough lawn in front of it, Charlotte Moberly noticed a middle-aged lady, with a quite pretty but unappealing face, sitting on a low seat on the grass seemingly engaged in sketching the trees before her.

> The woman wore a 'shady white hat, perched on a good deal of fair hair fluffed around her forehead . . . Her dress was long-waisted, with a good deal of fullness in the skirt, which seemed to be short. I thought she was a tourist, but that her dress was old-fashioned and rather unusual, though people were wearing fichu bodices that summer. I looked straight at her, but some indescribable feeling caused me to turn away annoyed at her being there.'

Miss Moberly and Miss Jourdain mounted some steps to the terrace in front of the house, and went towards the only one of its tall ground floor windows which was unshuttered, intending to take a look through it. Yet before they reached the window a youth darted out from a nearby doorway, banging the door closed behind him, and told them that if they wanted to get into the house they must enter via the front courtyard. And then, with a jaunty insouciance, he conducted them there. The two women, however, were then kept waiting in the foyer for the arrival of a large and happy French wedding party, and when they turned up they were all shown around it together by a guide. On completing this tour, they returned to the Hotel des Réservoirs at Versailles, where they had afternoon tea.

The women did not discuss in detail what they had seen that afternoon, simply because they were not aware that they had witnessed anything out of the ordinary. But some three months later, when Charlotte Moberly happened to mention the lady who had been sitting on the lawn in front of the Petit Trianon, she was startled to learn that her companion had no recollection of her being there. This seemed quite impossible to them both, as they had walked across the lawn together. Their incredulity grew when they discovered that Miss Moberly had not seen the woman and the girl on the farmhouse steps, who had been particularly noticed by Miss Jourdain, while Miss Jourdain had completely missed the woman Miss Moberly had seen shaking a duster at a window.

'Finding we had a new element of mystery,' commented Charlotte Moberly, 'and doubting how far we had seen any of the same things, we resolved to write down independent accounts of our expedition to Trianon, read up its history, and make every enquiry about the place.'

Then on 2 January 1902, about four and a half months afterwards and while she was on holiday, Eleanor Jourdain decided to revisit the Petit Trianon and its grounds alone. While there she had another strange experience. This began when she crossed a small bridge on her way to a group of buildings comprising the Hameau de la Reine, or hamlet of the Queen, which initiated the same depressed feeling in her -- 'as if I had crossed a line and was suddenly in a circle of influence' -- that both she and Miss Moberly had experienced before. Not long afterwards she came across a horse-drawn cart being filled with sticks by two labourers, who wore tunics and short capes with pointed hoods, the cape of one being red in colour, the other blue. Yet on glancing momentarily away from them, she found that when she looked back both they and their horse and cart were nowhere to be seen.

After she had walked around the Hameau, Miss Jourdain went on to the Orangerie, beyond which the path brought her to a thick wood. She followed the path through it, and was surprised to notice a man dressed in a cloak 'slip swiftly through the line of trees. The smoothness of his movement attracted my attention'. Not long afterwards the path divided into several branches, which confused her, but when she decided to follow one of them she heard the rustling of silk dresses and felt the presence of many people 'coming from behind and passing me' who spoke together in French, yet she saw no-one. When the invisible crowd had gone by, Miss Jourdain next heard, as if from a distance, the faint sound of light music being played. But then, to her surprise, the path she had taken returned her to the Orangerie, where she encountered a gardener 'who did not look like a Frenchman' and from whom she asked the way to the Queen's grotto. The man's directions, however, proved correct, for by taking the path he pointed out, Miss Jourdain walked by the Belvedere edifice to reach her destination with her normally buoyant feelings restored.

These very odd experiences undergone by the two English women started to make some sense to them when Eleanor Jourdain learned from friends that Marie Antoinette had apparently made her last visit to the Petit Trianon on 5 October 1789, and that, as she had sat in her grotto, a page had run to her carrying a letter containing the news that an angry mob was marching from Paris and would arrive in about one hour. Miss Jourdain also learned from a book about the Queen that a certain Comte de Vaudreuil, who had persuaded Her Majesty to take the part of Rosine in Caron de Beaumarchais's *The Barber of Seville* performed at the Trianon theatre, was of Creole birth and complexion and had had an ugly, pock-marked face. When Miss Jourdain later went to see the play at the Comedie Francais, she was struck by the fact that the Alguazils or Spanish gardeners in it were dressed in costumes almost identical to those worn by the two gardeners she and Miss Moberly had seen and from whom they had asked directions. But perhaps most remarkably, when Miss Moberly examined the portrait of the Queen painted by Wertmuller, the most lifelike painting of her, she realised that Her Majesty bore a strong resemblance to the lady she had seen sitting on the Petit Trianon lawn. She also read in the *Journal* of Madame Eloffe, Queen Marie Antoinette's milliner, that in 1789 she had washed and repaired several light, short summer skirts for her, and had made her two green silk bodices and several white fichus. And the woman on the lawn had worn such clothes.

These remarkable recollections and discoveries led Miss Moberly and Miss Jourdain to suspect that on the two days in question when they had been in Paris they had somehow briefly become part of a past event; that they had, in other words, undergone a time-slip. Their suspicions were confirmed when they revisited the Petit Trianon and its grounds on 4 July 1904, and again five days later on 9 July, when they discovered some unaccountable changes had taken place to certain of the buildings and to the landscape.

For example, the farmhouse outside which the woman and girl had stood had been replaced by a cottage; many of the paths, flower beds, and lawns were different; the kiosk or open-sided pavilion beside which the dark, ugly man had sat was gone, as was a nearby waterfall; the woods had been thinned out; the rough lawn no longer ran right up to the terrace of the Petit Trianon but stopped at a broad expanse of gravel in front of it; and the spot where the lady had sat sketching was occupied by a bush of ample growth and age. And in addition to the many other visitors, there were wooden garden seats everywhere, which made Miss Moberly comment: 'the common-place, unhistorical atmosphere was totally inconsistent with the air of silent mystery by which we had been so much depressed.'

Taken together, the evidence suggests that Charlotte Moberly and Eleanor Jourdain had a Past Encounter of the Third Kind together on 10 August 1901, which took them back into the late eighteenth century, some one hundred and twelve years before. This is not to say that they entered 'the present' as it was (and still is!) on 5 October 1789, for we cannot assume that the breathless, red-faced running man they encountered was the page who brought a message to Marie Antoinette on that date, even though the Queen may have then been on the Petit Trianon lawn and not in her grotto, where tradition says she was. But it was certainly one of the days immediately before the French revolution began. Miss Jourdain likewise appears to have undergone a similar, but seemingly incomplete time-slip on 2 January 1902, when she saw a different landscape and some apparently solid figures near the Petit Trianon, yet only heard the sounds made by others who apparently passed by her.

Such merging of 'the past' with 'the present' often involves a former building and its immediate surroundings, like the Petit Trianon and its associated paths and woods, becoming united with the witnesses' present in the form of a bubble, across whose invisible boundary one or more people may by chance walk, as did Charlotte Moberly and Eleanor Jourdain, and so find themselves in yesteryear, and sometimes indeed undergoing a negative mood change while doing so.

Such a remarkable regression in time also happened to a teenage girl named Edna May Hedges, as she cycled along the old Roman road named Ermine Street which runs close by the small village of Hannington, in north Wiltshire, where she lived, to Wanborough, situated about eight miles away, to visit her best friend one summer Sunday afternoon in the early 1930s. She had passed through the village of Stratton St Margarets and was approaching Lower Wanborough when the weather suddenly changed and a thunderstorm began, forcing her to seek shelter. The merging of two times which then ensued may even have been brought about in some way by the thunderstorm.

Fortunately Edna noticed a pretty thatched cottage standing down a side lane which offered her a refuge from the rain, and she quickly cycled to its gate, dismounted, and dashed through the rain-drops and the well-tended garden, to rap loudly on the cottage's door. The door, to her relief, was immediately and silently opened by an elderly, long-haired and grey-bearded man, whose clothing included a dark green waistcoat with bright metal buttons, and who smoked a pipe.

Edna breathlessly begged him for shelter, and the man, with a warm smile, beckoned her into the quaintly-furnished living room, where burning logs crackled out a welcome in the old-fashioned grate. However, the man's silence, despite his smile, made Edna feel awkward and intrusive, and she could not understand why no sound of the wind and the rain outside was audible in the room.

But what happened next was even more startling and perplexing for Edna, because without knowing how she got there, she suddenly found herself again cycling towards Wanborough, albeit beneath a clear sky. She had no recollection of either thanking or saying goodbye to the grey-bearded man, or indeed of leaving his lovely cottage.

The mystery deepened still further when, on arriving at Wanborough, Edna recounted her strange experience to her friend. The girl replied by saying that although Edna's dry clothes showed that she had taken shelter somewhere from the downpour of rain, she was surely mistaken about the pretty cottage, as all that stood at the place she described was a ruined cottage which had not been lived in for about 50 years!

And indeed, when Edna revisited the same turning the following weekend, she was astonished to discover that the cottage really was in a ruined state. The windows were broken and the thatch had fallen in, its interior was damp and empty, and the front garden was overgrown with weeds. And of course there was no sign whatsoever of the friendly, smiling man.

Another cyclist caught up in such an inexplicable event, which likewise seemed to involve a time-slip, was James Brown, a resident of Ipswich, in Suffolk. His remarkable experience happened, he told me, 'either in the Easter vacation of 1942 or early in the Long Vacation of the same year', when he was riding his bicycle from Ipswich to Cambridge, a 56-mile journey, a journey which initially took him along what is now the B1113 road, a trip he had done several times before, having become an undergraduate at St. John's College, Cambridge, in October 1941.

James said that he and a fellow St. John's College student, who also lived in Ipswich, 'would cycle both ways at the beginning and end of each term,' and he noted that, 'All signposts had been removed at the outbreak of war, but the route went directly through a number of places we knew, and was straightforward in between them.' However, his journey by bicycle on that occasion in 1942 was made alone because, having joined a small, inter-collegiate male-voice singing group, his presence in Cambridge was needed to take part in an audition the group was having with Leslie Woodgate, a BBC representative.

'I set out from Ipswich about 9 o'clock that morning,' James related. 'The roads were quiet, but this was not unusual as civilian travelling was discouraged in war time. The first place of any note was Needham Market, a largish village about 10 miles from Ipswich.'

The next settlement reached should have been the 'modest-sized town' of Stowmarket, four miles further on, but to James's bewilderment, he never reached it, despite him pedalling uninterruptedly along the familiar road.

> I cycled on through the uneventful countryside but Stowmarket failed to show itself,' he said. 'However, I had no option but to continue on the road I was already on -- there was no other. Nothing happened, and no-one appeared (but wartime would account for that) and this went on for a considerable time. At last I came to a higher point in the road, and looking down I saw the town of Bury St. Edmond's, which is 28 miles from Ipswich, and so half-way to Cambridge. The rest of my ride (through Newmarket) and my arrival at Cambridge were accomplished without further incident.
>
> He went on to say that 'a day or two after, I made the return journey, in the late afternoon and evening. On this occasion, I found Stowmarket in its usual place, and indeed was given a "Goodnight" by a resident.'

James still doesn't know what happened to Stowmarket on his outward journey, even though it was back where he expected it to be when he returned home. He recounted the puzzling absence of the town to his family and friends, and commented that

> My friend's father, who at that time was Deputy Chief Constable of E. Suffolk said I could not possibly have missed Stowmarket -- there was no other route I

could have taken.' His family, perhaps not surprisingly, humorously suggested that 'my dreamy mind had been on music' and that he simply failed to notice he was riding through Stowmarket, with which opinion James disagrees:

All I can say to this is that I was anxiously looking out for Stowmarket after leaving Needham Market and getting more and more puzzled, though I don't think alarmed. But I still recall an odd lifelessness about the scenery through which I was passing, even after over 60 years!

It is therefore possible that James Brown briefly and spontaneously rode into a 'past-present' before the town of Stowmarket was built, which would account for its absence, while still seeing and riding on the modern road, much as a horse-drawn coach and its driver and passengers encountered by Michael Higgins made a short sudden appearance into an afternoon in Hampshire in 1967.

The next fascinating case, which is the second time-slip account reported to me by Elizabeth of Malvern, also features a change in the quality of the ambient sound within a building belonging to a former time.

Elizabeth recounted that one summer's day in the early 1970s, she skipped work and went window shopping in the Shambles district of Worcester. The sun was warm and bright and the busy streets were noisy with the recorded music that seemingly blared out from every shop. She enjoyed the fun of it all and her search for bargains.

At last I'd had enough but before I went home I wanted to buy a present for our little dog, so I walked into a corn chandler's at the corner of the Shambles. I'd been in there before but today I was mildly surprised to find things had altered slightly.

Indeed, ahead of her, framed by an arch, was an inside entrance giving access to a room she had never seen before. It contained an enormous mahogany counter on which a large, old-fashioned mahogany cash-register stood and against which rested sacks of grain. The floor was made of wide unpolished wooden boards, and the shop shelves were not only sparsely filled, but the packaging of the goods lacked colour.

However, Elizabeth noticed in particular that

> The acoustics were amazing, making sounds so hushed that I could hear voices calling out in the street, while perhaps strangest of all was the apparent exterior rumble of wheels over cobblestones.
>
> Behind the counter sat a placid, smiling, elderly lady dressed in black with a white mob-cap and white apron. She was knitting busily and never spoke to me but she smiled and nodded pleasantly.

In her smiling silence the woman resembled the strange man encountered by Edna Hedges. However, when Elizabeth told her that she wanted to buy something nice for her dog, the lady obligingly reached up to a shelf and took down a card to which was attached a chew in the form of a rat. The creature was made of thin leather, and its body was plump with a filling consisting of small pieces of chopped, raw meat.

The card bore the name "Rawhide Rat" and the article's price, which was sixpence. The cerise-coloured lettering appeared to have been hand-printed.

Elizabeth knew as soon as she saw the rat that it was a perfect gift for her dog, and she happily handed over a sixpence piece for it. The woman took the coin without comment and dropped it into the cash register. Then Elizabeth happily went back out into the sunshine and the busy street, and made her way home, musing over the curious shop and its oddly silent, elderly assistant.

Her dog absolutely loved playing with and eating the Rawhide Rat, and Elizabeth resolved to buy him another when she next went into Worcester. Yet she did not think of keeping the 'Rawhide Rat' card with its amateurish printing, which went into the kitchen waste bin.

A month went by before Elizabeth found the time to return to the corn chandler in the Shambles. But she had a nasty shock when she passed through its front entrance. For the archway leading into the wood-floored, grain-scented room was no longer there: in its place was a solid wall.

Nonplussed, Elizabeth hurriedly found an assistant in the other part of the shop and asked her what had happened to the room and to the old lady. The girl stared at her blankly, then denied all knowledge of them. A male colleague was equally uncomprehending. As far as he knew, he said, the wall had always been there.

And when Elizabeth asked if the shop at least still sold Rawhide Rats, the man answered with a snort that it had never stocked such an item, whose uncooked meaty interior would certainly not be allowed.

Frowning distractedly, Elizabeth left the shop, feeling more puzzled and confused than she had ever been.

> I still regret throwing the Rawhide Rat's card away, because I am the only person that I have ever heard of who went through the curtain that divides two worlds and came back with a genuine concrete artefact.
>
> I also wish I had kept it because I truly believe, for a few precious moments, I entered the world of the Victorians and actually met a real one. This is not a ghost story. There was absolutely nothing ghostly about the plain practical shop or its occupant. They were solid and real.
>
> So maybe I was the intruder into another time, wearing my polyester mini-dress, dark glasses and long red hair. What did I look like to that elderly lady? Did she ever tell the people she knew about the strange woman dressed so oddly who paid with a coin dated far in advance of current money and with an unknown queen's head on it?

The apparent insouciance shown by inhabitants of the past to fashions of a future time, however, may be due more to their self-control and good manners than to an unthinking acceptance of them.

Yet when 12-year-old Carol Johnson entered a similar 'past-present' shop to Elizabeth's in 1954, while doing an errand for the aunt she was staying with in Saint John, Newfoundland, her modern gingham dress and brown leather Oxford shoes drew a disapproving stare from the lady already being served there, who wore a floor-length grey dress, black gloves and a black ruffled bonnet tied under her chin.

The white-aproned shopkeeper, whose shirt-sleeves were held up by armbands and who sported a large handlebar moustache and an eye visor, did not keep silent either. He asked Carol what she wanted and either bagged or wrapped in brown paper the grocery items she requested, and demanded 40 cents for them.

He also accepted without question the silver dollar she handed him, and he gave her two shiny new coins for her change, which, she later discovered, bore the date 1845.

When she left the store, Carol could not help noticing that its sign and the names it bore were different from those it had displayed when she had entered. This prompted her to run, startled by the odd discrepancy, back to her aunt's house, who was, of course, astonished to see the bright, new-looking 109-year-old coins (as they were in 1954) handed to her by Carol, although not startled enough to believe for a moment that her niece had actually been handed them as change in 1845.

And Carol, to her puzzlement and regret, like Elizabeth, never again found the old-world grocery store, despite often returning to the same intersection to look for it when she visited St John, and where stood a store with a different sign and name, whose interior was thoroughly modern and up-to-date. The shop had seemingly rejoined, like those other brief entrants into a twentieth-century present, the 'past-present' where it rightfully belonged.

A Past Encounter of the Second Kind happened to Brenda Collins, who lives in Cornwall, one Sunday in July 1975, when she and her first husband decided to go for an afternoon drive with their three children. It was a warm, sunny day, and the lovely blue sky was tempting enough by itself to prompt the excursion, although Brenda admits that the children would perhaps rather have stayed at home with their friends.

Once a route had been decided upon, they finally set off, with Brenda's husband driving, and headed towards

Weymouth. All went well as far as Brenda was concerned for the first hour or so, but then, at around three o'clock, 'a funny feeling' came over her and she began feeling a bit sick. She none the less bore her discomfort and hoped that it would soon pass.

> But then quite suddenly the main road changed into a narrow country lane, which I thought was rather odd, as I couldn't remember us going off on to another road. We went on further and came to a cross roads, or I thought we came to a cross roads, which had a big old oak tree standing on the opposite side.

They went on and drove past the intersection, and then Brenda suddenly saw a car coming towards them from the opposite direction. It was, she said, an old yellow-coloured car of 1930s' vintage, which while it was travelling somewhat to the right of them, Brenda realised with a start that there was not enough room for the two vehicles to pass one another. She cried out to her husband in alarm, telling him in no uncertain terms to slow down and to avoid the approaching yellow car.

However, her spouse was neither amused by nor glad of her warning, responding to her with a shouted, 'What are you on about, Brenda? There is no yellow car!' Brenda was both stunned and abashed when the car thereupon faded away, taking the danger with it, but the strange countryside remained visible around her. She said:

> We carried on down the same country lane for a little way and then my husband turned right, and as we did so the lane became like a track with grass growing in the middle. I turned to my husband and asked him where he was going, saying that I didn't like such very narrow lanes. 'Narrow lanes?' he loudly riposted. 'We're on a main road, for God's sake, Brenda, with white lines down the middle of it.' That stunned me, so I shut up and thought he must be thinking I am mad, which I was starting to think anyway.

According to Brenda, they next came to a thick expanse of trees on the left hand side of the lane, which gave her a really bad depressive feeling, and she pointed at them and expressed her disquiet. 'What trees?' asked her husband irritably, trying to keep his eyes on the road. 'Those in the forest over there,' she said. 'You are going mad,' he cried. 'Once and for all, Brenda, there are no country lanes and no trees here, only this main road and the houses beside it.'

> I was feeling very strange by this time, and wishing that the awful feeling would pass. But as I was driven by the trees, the feeling of dread worsened and I felt that someone may been murdered there a long time ago. But in a very short while, thank goodness, I was back and was seeing what everybody else was seeing: a wide main road with white lines down the middle and houses on each side of the road.

This suggests that Brenda was somehow able briefly to see through the divide which separated the present that she and her family were occupying and to look at the landscape which had previously existed there and to sense some of the darker emotions associated with it. Her experience was, in other words, a Past Encounter of the Second Kind.

By contrast, a woman living near Wells, in Somerset, recently wrote to tell me of a strange time-slip experience she had on a hot, humid night in September back in either 1973 or 1974 (she can't be certain of the exact year), when she resided at Biggin Hill, in Kent. It is different from the time-slips described previously in that only sounds were heard, but those were singular enough to suggest that she had 'eavesdropped' on a past event.

At around midnight on the night in question, my correspondent, being unable to sleep, had sat up in bed to read. But then, through the wide-open windows of her room, there suddenly came sounds which immediately caught her attention.

> The sounds which distracted me were those of a child's garden swing, squeaking in its to-ing and fro-

ing; and of children's chattering and laughter, soft laughter, excited at their play yet quietly contained somehow. I would like to emphasize that the laughter contained what I would call a beautiful quality, the like of which I'd never noticed before, and it was coming and fading, coming and fading, as if being carried to me and then away again on a gentle wind or breeze. But there was no gentle wind, nor breeze. The night was perfectly still with no air movement of any kind.

The noises, as far as my correspondent could determine, originated from the garden belonging to an elderly couple living opposite her, who she knew had neither children nor a swing. Yet when she went to the window to look out, the location of the sounds changed and 'now seemed to be coming, not from the garden, but all around the general vicinity, still with an intermittent coming and fading motion. It was not in the least eerie because it was so happy and lovely to listen to.'

During the next couple of days the woman made some inquiries about the sounds. She discovered that while the elderly couple who owned the garden from which she thought the sounds had come had heard nothing, the old woman who lived next door to her had heard them on several occasions. And this lady believed they came from the piece of waste ground that stood opposite her, next to the elderly couple's garden. It had once belonged, she said, to a London man who, in the 1930s, had built a wooden bungalow on it for weekend use. However, when the war started, he moved into the bungalow permanently to avoid the bombing, and during the Battle of Britain he brought his grandchildren out to stay with him for their safety. Then one afternoon, when the children were happily playing outside, a German Heinkel III bomber heading for RAF Biggin Hill prematurely released its payload of bombs, one of which fell on the man's plot, killing him and the children, and demolishing the bungalow.

My correspondent, who had previously noticed some rotting wooden boards and rusting iron chains, like those of a child's swing, lying on the waste plot, asked: 'I wonder if, what I heard on that humid Saturday night more than thirty years later, could have been some sort of supernatural recording or re-enactment of the events leading up to that fateful daylight raid all those years before?'

Yet the incident, as described, may well have been an auditory time-slip, and if it was, it was a repetitive Past Encounter of the Second Kind. Those who might claim that it was in reality a haunting should consider the possibility that any haunting is a time-slip of the Second Kind, but especially in this case, as any ghosts, in the absence of actual swings, would have considerable difficulty in producing the sounds made by them.

These remarkable cases reveal that on occasion ordinary, unsuspecting people can temporarily become part of a 'past present'. Yet those who undergo a Past Encounter of the Fourth Kind become 'time travellers' without generally experiencing any sense of movement, arriving in 'the past' at the same spot, and in a present that is as real to them as the one they apparently left. And if they can be seen by, and interact with, the people alive then, the situation is made more confusing by the fact that sometimes such perception as this does not happen.

Moreover, when someone from 'today' arrives among those living in a 'past present', he or she is, from their point of view, a visitor from the future. If such a visitor knew some history, it would enable him or her to warn those encountered about the problems and difficulties that lie ahead of them, and to suggest how they could be avoided. He or she might therefore be able to help change what happens, and thereby, at the same time, the course of events and our own present.

Now it so happens that there are many examples in history of important people like kings and emperors being advised by Seers or by fortune-tellers to avoid doing some particular act and so avoid its unfortunate consequences, even though those so warned invariably fail to heed the advice given. This naturally suggests that when a future event is observed by a Seer, changing it for the better is not easy, which is why we often speak of the immutability of fate. And while instances of someone using a Past Encounter of the Fourth Kind to alter history are for obvious reasons rare, the following may well be such an example.

The night before the battle of Flodden Field on 9 September 1513, King James IV of Scotland, accompanied by his knights and servants, attended the evensong service at the kirk of St Michael at Linlithgow. While the king was at prayer an old man entered the church. He was distinguished by having a high forehead and amber-coloured, shoulder-length hair, a beautiful long azure-blue robe girded at the waist, and a 'comely and very reverend' mien. The striking newcomer asked where the king was pewed, and on being shown his location, pushed his way through the throng to James, then leaned over those flanking him to say gravely to the king:

> Sire, I am sent hither to entreat you to delay your expedition for this time, and proceed no further in your intended journey; for if you do, you shall not prosper in your enterprise, nor will any of your followers do so. I am further charged to warn you, not to use the acquaintance, company, or counsel of women, as you tender your honour, life, and estate.

The old man then stepped back into the crowded nave and left the astonished monarch behind him. However, immediately after the service, James ordered the man to be brought to him, for he wished to question him further and to learn more, but discovered, much to his dismay, that he could not be found, despite numerous members of his entourage having seen him and marked him closely, although none could say how, when or where he left them. He had simply disappeared as mysteriously as he had arrived.

None the less, despite the warning given to him, King James continued with his ill-fated march into England, and when he crossed the Tweed, Thomas Howard, the Earl of Surrey, hurriedly marched north with his English forces to intercept him. The two armies met at Flodden Field in the Cheviot Hills, where the Scots, perhaps mindful of the prophecy made to their king, advanced upon the English in perfect silence, as if aware they were going to their doom. And although they fought with the utmost bravery and pressed the English hard, their resolution broke when King James was killed as he tried to reach the English standard. The remainder of the battle was a rout, and when the day was over ten thousand Scots, including the flower of their nobility, lay dead on that grim plain.

Because James's son, also named James, was only an infant at the time, his widow Margaret succeeded him. But the following year (1514) she married the Earl of Angus, who was made regent in her stead. This led the Earl, with his wife's connivance and help, to prevent James from ever acceding to the throne, and he was eventually driven to imprison the teenage prince, who remained behind bars for three years until he escaped in 1528 to gain finally his birthright. Hence it was by the Queen's actions that the second part of the prophecy proved true.

The amber-haired, blue-robed, aged man may therefore have come from 'the future', in which case he was, like Flavius Mantus, a 'whole body' time-shifter, although one who was a messenger of another or others, as he said that he was *sent* to warn the monarch not to proceed. This notion, fantastic though it may seem, is supported by his sudden and enigmatic arrival and departure, and by the fact that he was unknown to those local people within the church. His appearance also closely matches that of other time-shifters whom I shall discuss later.

We do not know how time-slips occur, but as 'whole body' Encounters of the Fourth Kind can happen spontaneously, then it might perhaps be possible to induce them, either by creating the right conditions or by developing the necessary mental techniques. If so, this would open up a field of exploration that is almost impossible to imagine or comprehend.

CHAPTER FIVE

CLUES IN THE ROCKS

Him God beholding from his prospect high
Wherein past, present, and future he beholds,
Thus to his only Son foreseeing spake

From *Paradise Lost*, by John Milton

At the beginning of the French Arthurian romance known as *Queste del Saint Graal* (or 'The Quest of the Holy Grail'), a great stone is depicted as floating down the river running by Camelot and then coming to rest on one of its banks. King Arthur and his barons hurry out to examine the wonder, and they find that 'held fast in the red marble was a sword, superb in its beauty, with a pommel carved from a precious stone cunningly inlaid with letters of gold'.

The inscription on it tantalizingly announces: 'None shall take me hence but he whose side I am to hang. And he shall be the best knight in the world.' This prompts several knights to try to remove the sword from the stone, but only one manages to do so, namely Galahad, who 'took hold of the sword and drew it as easily from the stone as if it had never been fast'.

We are not, unfortunately, told how the sword came to be in the red marble stone, although presumably 'magic' had once placed it there. Magic is a convenient explanation for such wonders, particularly where the world of myth and fairy is concerned.

But none the less, what are we to make of the following news item which appeared in a Scottish newspaper, *The Kelso Chronicle*, dated 31 May 1844?

> A few days ago, as some workmen were employed in
> quarrying a rock close to the Tweed, about a quarter

of a mile below Rutherford Mill, a gold thread was discovered in the stone at a depth of eight feet. How long this remnant of a former age has remained in the situation from which it was taken, will baffle the skill of the antiquary or geologist to determine. A small bit of the thread has been sent to our office for the inspection of the curious.

Kelso is a small town standing on a bend of the river Tweed, about seven and a half miles as the crow flies from the border with England, in what was, in 1844, the county of Roxburgh. Rutherford Mill is not marked on modern maps, although the village of Rutherford is. It lies about six miles west of Kelso and three quarters of a mile south of the Tweed, so Rutherford Mill would once have stood nearby on the river.

We do not know why the rock in question was being quarried a short way downstream from Rutherford Mill or what sort of rock it was. But as any workable outcrops of Caledonian granite lie far from Kelso, and because a length of gold thread is more likely to have been noticed and recovered from a rock that was split rather than blasted, we can perhaps surmise that the thread was embedded in a sedimentary rock, not an igneous one.

Sedimentary rocks are formed from water-eroded sediments brought down by streams and rivers, which settle out and accumulate in their beds and estuaries, or out to sea, and which are gradually compacted by their own weight into rock. This process not only takes a long time, but it also takes a long time for sedimentary strata to be exposed at the surface by uplift and by weathering, which means that the rock in which the gold thread was found was many millions or perhaps even hundreds of millions of years old.

How then did the thread get into the rock? If we discount its intrusion by supernatural means, there is really only one explanation: it must have fallen into a river or sea when the sediments were being laid down. The thread was then covered by further sediments, which thickened as time went by and which were, in due course, compressed into rock. And if that happened, the thread must have been dropped there long before human beings evolved and gold thread was made.

That, of course, sounds impossible, although if we consider that someone having loose gold thread about them was time-slipped into the distant past and who then dropped it into water, the impossible becomes the possible

However, if the reader thinks it is more likely that the quarrymen were mistaken in believing that the gold thread came from the rock, or that the whole business was a hoax, the experience of Mrs S W Culp, who found a length of chain in a lump of coal, might be sufficiently convincing.

Mrs Culp's remarkable discovery took place outside her suburban home in Morrisonville, Illinois, early in June 1891, when she was breaking up some large pieces of coal preparatory to filling the coal scuttle. On cracking apart one particular outsize lump, a length of chain suddenly emerged from it, much to her surprise.

> At first Mrs Culp thought the chain had been dropped accidentally in the coal (noted the reporter for the *Morrisonville Times*), but (when) she undertook to lift the chain up, the idea of its having been recently dropped was at once made fallacious, for as the lump of coal broke, it separated almost in the middle, and the circular position of the chain placed the two ends near to each other; and as the lump separated, the middle of the chain became loosened while each end remained fastened to the coal.

Coal is formed from the plants which grew in the hot, steamy swamps and river valleys of very ancient times, and which were later overlaid by sedimentary deposits and thus compressed into the black, ignitable rock we know today. But whereas some types of coal date from the more recent middle or early Tertiary era, Illinois coal was formed during the Carboniferous age, which lasted from about 350 million to 270 million years ago, and which therefore makes the lumps Mrs Culp broke up extremely ancient.

There were no human beings in existence two hundred and seventy or more million years ago, nor were there any creatures able to have manufactured chains (or gold thread). That being so, it is impossible to account for the presence of such a chain within a lump of coal unless it was taken back to that early time from 'the present' either by spontaneous movement or by a time-slipping individual.

Now it may be thought that the Carboniferous age is simply too long ago for anyone to seriously believe that anything or anybody could go there. However, let me again point out that the past moment when the chain (or the gold thread or even the people who might have carried them) materialized is not 'back there' in the sense that, say, a mountain from which we are travelling is left miles behind us. There is in fact no distance at all between that 'past present' or any other, for that matter, and the one you are enjoying now. For as we have seen, the whole of reality participates in a timeless Oneness, and despite the difficulty of time-slipping, once it is achieved it is no harder to step into Carboniferous times than it is into last week, or into what we call 'the future.'

Not long after the gold thread turned up in that rock near Rutherford Mill, another anomalous object was found in a geological specimen at Springfield, Massachusetts, USA. The discovery took place in December 1851, and it was reported by the local *Springfield Republican* newspaper, whose man-on-the-spot wrote:

> Hiram de Witt, of this town, who has recently returned from California, brought with him a piece of auriferous quartz rock, about the size of a man's fist. On Thanksgiving-day it was brought out for exhibition to a friend, when it accidentally dropped upon the floor and split open. Near the centre of the mass was discovered, firmly embedded in the quartz and slightly corroded, a cut-iron nail, the size of a six-penny nail. It was entirely straight, and had a perfect head. By whom was that nail made? At what period was it planted in the yet un-crystallized quartz? How came it to California?

Auriferous means 'gold bearing', which suggests that Hiram de Witt had taken part in the famous California gold rush of 1849, when tens of thousands of people from all parts of the

United States flocked to the state to dig for gold. The quartz rock was therefore probably a memento brought home by the intrepid de Witt, one that he proudly showed to visitors eager to hear of his adventures, which they certainly would have done if he had been lucky enough to find gold and make some money.

Mining in the early 19th century

It was quite by chance that the auriferous quartz rock was dropped and broken, and it was fortuitous that the one de Witt brought home contained an iron nail. And the nail, according to the newspaper account, was embedded in the quartz at its centre, which means that it must have been in situ before the quartz crystallized around it. Hence the nail, a manufactured item, was lying where it could not possibly have been, if conventional thinking is correct, all those many millions of years ago.

In 1844 another short nail was discovered embedded in a block of sandstone nine inches thick at the Kingoodie quarry in Perthshire, Scotland and which had been brought up from a depth of several feet. The underground rock structure at the quarry consisted of alternating bands of Devonian sandstone separated by a type of boulder clay known as 'till'. The Devonian period preceded that of the Carboniferous.

According to Sir David Brewster (1781-1868), the eminent geologist who investigated the matter and wrote paper about it, the nail head and one inch of its shaft were embedded in the Devonian sandstone while the remainder, which included the point, projected into the overlying till. The latter, and shortest, part of the nail was almost completely corroded away with rust, yet the portion within the rock was as bright and shiny as the day it was made.

But if these anomalous artefacts are sufficiently challenging in themselves to science, what are we to make of the two manufactured objects described below, which were both extracted from coal and which are surely as indicative of time-slipping as the chain found by Mrs Culp?

One day in 1885, at the Braun foundry in Schöndorf, Austria, a worker was startled to notice an odd, pitted yet regular-shaped metal object lying within the large lump of brown lignite coal he had just split in two. The lignite itself had been mined at Wolfsegg am Hausruck. He chipped the strange item free and found it was about three finger-widths broad and long, with a rounded upper and lower surface, and two finger-widths deep, while encircling its 'waist' was a deep groove. Indeed, the strange object's overall geometric shape turned out to be, as the accompanying diagrams show, an oblate spheroid, although it had evidently been specially worked to alter its 'natural' circular circumference into that of a rough square.

Later chemical analysis by Dr Adolf Gurit and others at the Salzburg museum, where it was eventually put on display and where it gained the misleading name of 'the Salzburg Cube', showed it to consist of an alloy of iron and carbon, plus a small quantity of admixed nickel, and weighed 785 grams or just over one and a half pounds. It is a very peculiar artefact indeed, evidently made from cast-iron and thus of human manufacture, and one that should not have been present in a lump of lignite coal.

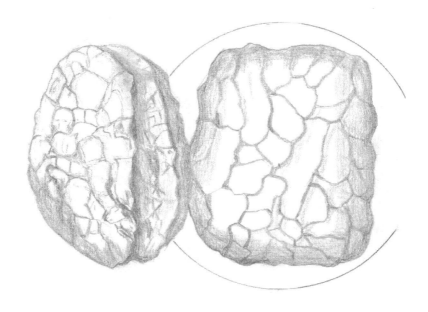

The "Salzburg Cube" (picture by the author)

However, neither Dr Gurit nor his colleagues could determine what the object actually was, as none of them had ever seen anything like it before. So we can only wonder from where it originated and whether it was a separate object in its own right or was instead part of a larger device, perhaps a machine of some sort. Its rough, pitted outer surface is also unusual, although the groove around it suggests to me that it was used either as a weight to keep a loop of cord taught or as a missile if the cord was employed as a sling.

But we do know that the lignite coal seam from which it came was of Tertiary age, and thus had a median age of about 30 million years. This naturally suggests that the object had been time-slipped, although as it could not be identified when it was recovered or at any time since, it almost certainly came from 'the future'. And as with the other time-slipped objects, we cannot tell if it underwent a spontaneous time shift or if it was taken back into the Miocene or Oligocene by someone who accidentally dropped it on to the soggy ground of a Tertiary coal forest.

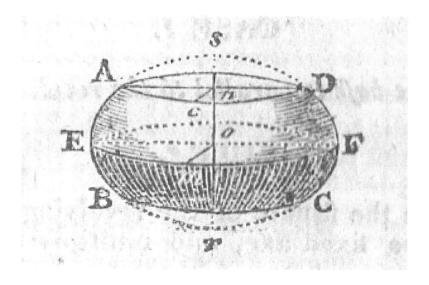

An oblate spheroid

One of the most intriguing and poignant time-slipped objects came to public attention in 1901, when it was briefly reported in *The Strand Magazine* that 'Mr R C Hardman, of Meadhurst, Uppingham, has been the fortunate finder of a coin dated 1397 embedded in a lump of coal, which formed part of a ton of that useful commodity bought at current prices.'

This short description was accompanied by a photograph of the lump of coal, which had been broken in two, like those previously mentioned, and which showed the coin lying face up in the perfectly circular cavity where it had lain for unimaginable eons. As the coal Mr Hardman bought would certainly have been mined locally, either in Rutland itself or in adjacent Leicestershire or Nottinghamshire, it was of Carboniferous age, and would mean that the coin had been encased in the coal for at least 270 million years.

The coin may of course have been spontaneously time-slipped back that far, or it may have gone along with, and been dropped by, an unknown medieval Englishman, who was time-slipped from 1397 (or thereabouts) and vanished into a nightmare. For at one moment he was perhaps sauntering along Uppingham High Street and in the next he found himself squelching through a Carboniferous coal forest, frightened beyond belief and no doubt believing, feeling as he did the heat of the humid air and glimpsing the great, ugly flesh-eating amphibians among the ferns, horsetails and scale trees, that he had been carried off by demons into Hell.

We should not be surprised that many of the artefacts mentioned above were found in coal because this is the rock type mined in by far the largest quantities. Much of the coal was burned to heat homes throughout the northern hemisphere in the nineteenth and twentieth centuries, where it came under the relatively close scrutiny of millions of people who filled their scuttles with it and who often had to break lumps of it up.

But even more incredible and challenging to science is the article that appeared in *The Midland and Rugby Gazette*, of Saturday, February 23, 1901, which reported:

> On Friday evening last Mr Clarke, manager to Messrs. Neudegg and Sons, of North Street, Rugby, had a most curious find. A large lump of coal had been smouldering upon his fire for more than an hour when in order to make the fire burn more brightly he smashed the coal with the poker, and, to his great astonishment, out rolled a toad. As quickly as possible the reptile was rescued from the flames, and was found to be alive. At first the toad was unable to move, but, by degrees, it acquired some slight use of his limbs. Upon a more minute examination being made, the toad was found to have no mouth, the aperture appearing to be perfectly sealed up, as also is the rectum. At first no eyes were visible but the latter organs have since developed, but the orbs are apparently sightless, various tests having been

applied to arrive at a decision on the point. When first discovered it was quite black in colour, but after having been placed in water it has assumed a speckled appearance. In size it is not quite as large as a full-grown toad, and its fore limbs are not quite perfect in shape, though its long imprisonment in the coal from which it was so curiously released may account in some measure for the deformity.

The toad was at first placed in a box, but when seen by a representative of *The Midland Times* it was in a glass jar, and although its mouth was sealed there was a perceptible and regular movement of its throat, as though it was in the act of breathing and swallowing. In the position where the nostrils would (normally) be found were two small holes, very little bigger than the point of a pin, and, apparently, it was through these small holes that all air inhaled had to be drawn.

It is undoubtedly a most extraordinary find, and it is a matter of regret that the piece of coal in which the toad must have reposed for so many centuries could not have been preserved, showing the cavity in which it had existed. Having been on the fire, however, for so long, on being struck by the poker, fell to pieces, and it was by the merest chance that the toad was found.

It is perhaps unnecessary to mention that a toad is not a reptile but an amphibian or that the toad in question must have been entombed in the coal for far longer than the 'many centuries' mentioned. And this discovery of a living toad in a large piece of coal at Rugby, in Warwickshire, is by no means the first such anomalous find. In fact *The Gentleman's Magazine* of April 1773 mentions that on March 16th of that year, at the Lathum coal-works in Lancashire, 'a large toad was found alive in a solid coal 180 feet underground. On being exposed to the air, it instantly died.'

The animal group known as amphibians did not fully evolve until towards the end of the Carboniferous Period, and the common ancestor of those with which we are familiar today, namely frogs, toads, salamanders and newts, did not appear until about the middle of the following geological period, the Permian, while frogs and toads themselves only evolved in the succeeding Triassic period. Hence the relatively late appearance of such amphibians in the geological record, means that those found encased in Carboniferous coal must have been time-slipped back there. And such time-slipping does not only affect toads, as the following report in the *Glasgow Herald* of 1838 reveals:

> A few days since there was found in one of the pits at Kilmarknock Colliery, imbedded in coal, 130 feet from the surface, a frog, which, on being liberated, immediately began to use its long-lost liberty and leap about. The bed of the animal, closely resembling its shape, was clearly discerned in the coal from which it was extricated. We have heard of toads being found in similar situations, but never before an animal of this kind. When discovered it was almost as black as the diamond in which it was entombed; but by being handled and exposed to the air for some time, it became much lighter in colour, and appeared little different from ordinary animals of the same species, with the exception that its legs were longer in proportion to the bulk of the body.

An even earlier discovery of a time-slipped frog was reported on October 4th 1818:

> As Joseph Madelen, a miner, employed in South Moor colliery, near Medmomsley, in the county of Durham, was hewing at a solid stratum of coal, about 6 feet in thickness, and 13 fathoms (i.e. almost eighty feet) from the surface of the earth, he found a frog inclosed in the solid mass, which, immediately on being liberated, began to exercise the function of animal life. The recess in the coal in which it was found, was exactly fitted to its body, and apparently had no communication whatever with the surface of the block. The animal was exactly the colour of the coal, but on being put into a vessel of water, its sooty covering disappeared, and it appeared speckled like

the rest of its species.

But what is even more curious is that coal is not the only rock type in which toads have been found alive. When workmen at a quarry called Byker Hill, near Newcastle, split apart a three ton block of freestone, on November 18th 1812, they released a living toad in the middle of it, and 'the cavity that contained the animal, to which there was no passage, was the model of its figure, and was lined with a black substance, suffused with moisture.'

An earlier discovery of a living toad found immured rock was mentioned in *The Gentleman's Magazine* dated July 1748, in which a correspondent writes to say that 'Sir, I saw in Staffordshire, in my way to this place, the cavity in a stone, which being lately broken a toad came out alive: the stone was solid, and I could see no manner of perforation by which the animal could breathe or take in the outward air.'

We are left, unfortunately, with no record of what type of stone it was that contained the toad, although it almost certainly will have been sedimentary in origin.

An even earlier reference to a similarly rock-bound toad was made by Ambrose Paré (1510-90), the chief surgeon to Henry III, king of France, who wrote that

> Being at my seat, near the village of Meudon, and overlooking a quarry-man, whom I had set to break some very large and hard stones, in the middle of one we found a huge toad, full of life, and without any visible aperture by which it could get there. I began to wonder how it received birth, had grown and lived; but the labourer told me, it was not the first time he had met with a toad, and the like creatures, within huge blocks of stone, and no visible opening or fissure.

A letter from a correspondent to the editor of *Notes and Queries* magazine, dated April 29, 1865, is made doubly interesting by him not only stating the rock type in which the toad was found and the circumstances of its discovery, but by his description of the animal itself.

During the excavations which are being carried out under the superintendence of Mr James Yeal, of Dyke House Quay, in connection with the Hartlepool Water Works, the workmen yesterday morning found a toad, embedded in a block of magnesium limestone, at a depth of twenty-five feet from the surface of the earth, and eight feet from any spring-water vein. The block of stone had been cut by a wedge, and was being reduced by workmen, when a pick split open the cavity in which the toad had been incarcerated. The cavity was no larger than its body, and presented the appearance of being a cast of it . . .

The toad is in the possession of Mr S. Horner, the President of the Natural History Society, and continues in as lively a state as when found. On minute examination, its mouth is found to be completely closed, and the barking noise it makes proceeds from its nostrils. The claws of its fore feet are turned inwards, and its hind ones are of extraordinary length, and unlike the present English toad.

The amateur geologist who found the toad, the Rev. Robert Taylor, comments that 'I am still ready to maintain that the animal must have been alive in the dormant state since the deposition of the material of the rock,' which he identifies as being magnesium limestone,

Dr Robert Plot, the author of *The Natural History of Staffordshire*, published in 1686, and the keeper of the Ashmolean Museum and Professor of Chemistry at Oxford, reveals that in Staffordshire toads 'have been frequently found close imprison'd within the middle of solid blocks of Stone' and names the places where such remarkable discoveries have been made, which include Horton, Knypersley, Ingestre, and the village of Brocton, and he goes on to say:

But the *Toad* that was found in the most astonishing manner, certainly that ever was heard of, was that at *Statfold*, if the tradition they have of it be true, where as the story goes, the *Steeple* being to be taken down to prevent falling, the top-stone of the *Spire* or *Pinnacle* being taken off, was thrown down whole into the *Church-yard*, but breaking in its fall, there appear'd a *living Toad* in the Center of it, which (as most of the rest are said to do) died quickly after it was exposed to the Air.

A toad was also found alive on the property of a Mr Bathurst, a manufacturer of earthenware pots, in a thick layer of clay at the village of Benthall, Shropshire, on September 23rd, 1855. It was unearthed about five and a half feet below the surface of the ground, when the clay was being dug out from beneath a thin bed of feruginous coal.

The spade fortunately brought up the clod without injuring its inhabitant. As might be expected, for some time he was very impatient of light, which appeared to distress him greatly, but by degrees he became accustomed to it. When I saw him his eyes were as brilliant as possible, his skin moist, and of a full olive green, and his mouth hermetically sealed.

But while many toads, remarkably enough, have been found fully encased in sedimentary rocks such as freestone, limestone and marble, they are by no means the only creatures to have been similarly retrieved. My research has shown that the list of rock-encased animals also includes newts, shell fish, worms, an adder, crayfish, and perhaps most remarkably of all, two live dogs. The latter's discovery was recorded by the medieval chronicler, William of Newburgh (1136-98):

On splitting a vast rock, with wedges, in a certain quarry, there appeared two dogs, but, without any spiracle whatever, filling up the cavity of the rock which contained them. They seemed of that species which are called harriers, but of fierce countenance, disagreeable smell, and without hair. They report that one of them soon died: but that the other, having a most ravenous appetite, was for many days fondled by

Henry, bishop of Winchester.

The latter was Henry of Blois, brother of King Stephen, who became bishop in 1129, and died 1171.

The two dogs were certainly time-slipped, as dogs, being the descendants of grey wolves, did not evolve until about 100,000 years ago, and the breed called harriers are much more recent.

Equally curiously, three live newts were found encased in a lump of chalk extracted from the bed of a chalk-pit, which was being examined for fossils by the eminent geologist Edward Daniel Clarke in 1817. Two of them died soon after being released from their calcareous home, but the third newt actively revived on being placed in some water, to the extent that it managed to escape recapture. When Dr Clarke and the friend who owned the chalk-pit collected newts from the local area for comparison, they found that none resembled the three found, which seemingly confirmed that the chalk-bound newts belonged to an ancient, extinct species.

And just as remarkable are the comments made about the travertine quarry at Tivoli, in Italy, where the stones for many Roman buildings such as the Coliseum, were cut, by Francois Misson, who says:

> The Stones of Tivoli put me in mind of a memorable accident related by Alexander Tassoni in his *Various Thoughts*. Not many Days ago, says that Author, the Workmen that were employed to dig at Tivoli, having cleft a great Mass, found in the Middle of it an empty Space, in which there was a living Crayfish, that weighed four Pounds, which they boiled and did eat.

The above-mentioned Alexandro Tassoni (1565-1636), was an Italian poet and writer, who published his ten books on *Diverse* (or *Various*) *Thoughts,* in 1620.

The anomalous objects and animals found in coal and in other types of rock were discovered quite by chance, and if, as I suspect, they represent a small fraction of time-slipped objects or creatures waiting to be discovered, I can but hope that interested readers will devote some time to examining rocky outcrops in their locality. Any partly visible find must, if possible, be removed with its surrounding rocky envelope, and examined thus encased by scientists before being extracted from the rock. The discovery will only then be regarded as genuine, and scientists will be obliged to explain how such a thing could happen, which will effectively overthrow the whole present edifice of science. The entombed object will become of priceless value.

Regarding non-living objects, I have thus far mentioned the discovery in coal and other rocks two nails, one piece of gold thread, one length of chain, one coin dated 1397, and a strange metal cube of unknown function. Other anomalous finds include a quantity of gold and silver coins that were released from a flint nodule when it was flung at a rock in a quarry at Chute Forest near Stonehenge, Hampshire, by a young game beater. Some sixty-five coins were recovered, and when later examined by experts the coins turned out to have been minted in the Channel islands during the fourth century BC. They must somehow have been time-slipped together.

A similar monetary treasure trove was released from a smashed lump of flint found in a quarry at Westerham in Kent. The several coins were identified as Gallic in origin and dated from between 150 to 50 BC. Both discoveries took place, as far as I can ascertain, in the 1930s. We can again only wonder if the coins had been independently time-slipped into 'the past' or had been moved there along with their owner.

And likewise, during a blasting operation at a quarry at Dorchester, Massachusetts in 1851, the explosion ejected from the sedimentary rock a four and a half inch high bell-shaped metal vase. This curious object was beautifully decorated with fern-like plants inlaid in silver and was obviously made by a highly skilled craftsman, yet the culture from which it originated has not been identified.

All these various items, including possibly the oblate spheroid, while definitely man-made, are low-technology objects, and date from between the fourth-century BC and the nineteenth century AD. The metal spheroid, however, is probably of an earlier date, although it might have come, like the bell-shaped vase, from what is to us 'the future' or from another dimension or time-channel altogether.

However, in 1961, the three owners of the LM&V Gem and Gift Shop in Olancha, California, namely Wally Lane, Mike Mikesell, and Virgina Maxey, stumbled across something far more technically advanced when they sawed through a geode they had picked up in the Coso mountains, east of Lake Owens. Geodes are small rocks that contain an interior cavity in which colourful crystals and minerals have formed, and the trio had hoped that the one they had found would sell for a good price.

But the gem collectors were disappointed to find that the cavity of the fist-sized geode contained no crystals. Rather, it held an apparently man-made object that was later shown to consist of a central metal rod one tenth of an inch in diameter surrounded by a ceramic casing, which was in turn enclosed by a hexagonal envelope made of petrified wood. And the mysterious object was so tough that Mike Mikesell's diamond saw blade broke when he tried to cut through it.

The three store-owners had X-ray photographs taken of the geode, and when the photographs were sent to Paul Willis, the editor of *INFO Journal*, he immediately noted that the artefact closely resembled an automobile sparking plug. The geode was also examined by a professional geologist, who determined from the fossils present in the casing of sedimentary rock that it was about half a million years old. Now how a sparking plug, if that's what it actually is, got into a geode of that age is seemingly completely inexplicable, although if the object had been spontaneously time-slipped back half a million years, or alternatively dropped by someone who had undergone the same amazing translocation, it could have become surrounded by, and thus protected by, such an envelope of rock. This would seem to be the only possible solution to the mystery.

The last case I want to discuss is in its way the most incredible and intriguing of all, especially when we remember that those people who have undergone a time-slip into 'the past' usually saw events that happened at the same location. This further suggests that objects which undergo a spontaneous time-slip will remain in situ, and that if they turn up again, they will be found where they originally disappeared. As we shall see, this presents us with a seemingly insoluble paradox.

But first some more geology. Water-borne sediments may sometimes harden into rock around animal bones or woody plant parts, which then dissolve away leaving hollows in the rock retaining their exact shape. Later, these moulds may become filled by minerals like iron sulphide and calcite, or even by semi-precious crystals of quartz, opal or agate, to form much-valued mineralized fossil casts. These casts are comparatively rare, and they do. of course, take a very long time to form.

In 1787 men quarrying limestone for the construction of a new court house or *palais de justice*, just outside Aix-en-Provence in southern France, began digging through a layer of sandstone at a depth of about 45 feet to reach the next, and 12th, band of limestone rock, whereupon they found, much to their astonishment, the handles of hammers and other tools, petrified in agate, that were the exact replicas of the wooden ones they were using themselves. But that wasn't all. The sandstone also contained flat, broken fragments of inch-thick agate, which the quarrymen discovered could be fitted together like pieces of a jig-saw to form a petrified board between seven and eight feet long and eighteen inches wide, with rounded wavy edges, that had precisely the same dimensions and shape as their own wooden quarrymen's boards. And just as incredibly, these petrified versions of their own implements lay in the sand among portions of limestone columns and other half-worked pieces of masonry identical in design to the ones then being carved elsewhere in the quarry!

Limestone and chalk are formed from the calcium carbonate skeletons or tests of microscopic marine organisms known as foraminifera which were abundant in the warm seas of Cretaceous times. When the tiny animals died their skeletons fell to the sea bottom in a continuous 'rain', to form beds of ever-increasing thickness which, in due course, compacted under their own weight into rock. The limestone quarried near Aix-en-Provence, which was laid down in the shallow sea that once covered the region, is therefore about 100 million years old. And this means, if we discount the possibility of a hoax, which would have been extremely difficult, if not impossible, for anyone to have carried out, that the tools, along with the associated pieces of masonry, must have somehow intruded themselves 45 feet below the 'modern' ground level and then remained there undisturbed for eons while petrification occurred, before they were discovered in 1787.

So how did they get there? There is really only one answer that fits all the facts, namely that the tool handles, the board, and the chunks of worked and unworked limestone, were spontaneously time-slipped from the quarry of the late 1780s and 'back' 100 million years or thereabouts, where they appeared at the same spot on the sandy beach that then covered the area. They were gradually covered by either wind-blown or high-tide deposited sand, and then submerged with the beach, when either the sea level rose or the land subsided. The beach in this way became the bed of a shallow sea and was covered by a layer of ooze derived from the calcium carbonate shells of dead foraminifera, a process which was repeated eleven (or possibly more) times during the following millions of years, and which in turn resulted in the sand becoming compacted into sandstone and the ooze into limestone. While that was happening the wooden handles and the board dissolved away, leaving cavities behind in which crystals of agate grew and so formed casts of them. Then after lying entombed in the layer of sandstone, sandwiched between beds of limestone, for 100 million years, the casts and the limestone blocks were dug up in the quarry from which the original handles, board, and the stone blocks, had come!

But clearly, time-slipped objects that become encased in rock present us with a paradox. For when the rock moves into 'the present' containing the object, there will be two of them, one in the rock and its twin in the place where it is kept. Even more paradoxically, the rock-bound object could theoretically be found before the date of its own manufacture!

This is not a problem where the agate casts are concerned, as they merely retain the shape of the time-slipped handles and board, yet the blocks of stone and carved columns found with them must have been duplicated.

However, the existence of two copies of the same object is not as impossible as it seems. Physicists have detected such unusual 'twinning' at sub-atomic levels, and doubles or doppelgangers of people (and their clothing) have been reported throughout history. Hence the simultaneous existence of two nails that are the same nail, or two stones, coins or anything else, could also occur.

Yet remarkably, there is no report of any tool handles or a board, or pieces of worked and unworked limestone (which were large in size), mysteriously vanishing from the quarry of 1787, which must have happened if the items had been physically time-shifted from there. This may mean that the quarry from which they came and in which they were found after being buried for 100 million years is paradoxically both the same quarry and not the same quarry. There are, in other words, two versions of it, both of which exist in the year we call 1787: one from which the tool handles, board and limestone blocks mysteriously vanish, and another in which these same items or their casts are dug up. And if there are two identical quarries, then there must be two identical sets of quarrymen and two almost identical worlds wherein those quarries and quarrymen exist.

If so, there are also two or perhaps even more versions of you, me and everybody else, who live in parallel worlds, that are entirely separate yet somehow intimately connected. We apparently live in the world where the items mentioned above are discovered buried in sandstone. Our other selves exist in the one where they disappear, and the other you, of course, will have just finished reading the same chapter in an almost identical book, although you will have read about how objects mysteriously vanished at the quarry in the parallel version of Aix-en-Provence!

Finally, the great Swiss chronicler Johann Stumpf (1500-1578) mentions in his *Schwytzer Chronika* (1554) that near Berne, in the year 1460, the workmen at a metal ore quarry uncovered, to their astonishment, at a depth of about 300 feet, a ship containing the carcases of 48 men, along with many other items like anchors, oars, knives for eating, and so forth.. The find was also recorded by his admirers, namely the Antwerp-born Abraham Ortel (1527-98) and Josias Simler (1530-78), who both had encouraged Stumpf to publish the first edition of his famous chronicle, which he did in 1548.

It is impossible, at this late date, to say more about this incredible find, except to wonder at it and to postulate that the vessel and its occupants must have been unaccountably time-shifted back many tens of millions of years, upon which distant lost shore the ship foundered to be quickly swamped by sediment, and thereby preserved with its crew, for later discovery, encased in solid rock.

CHAPTER SIX

THE FOOTSTEPS OF TIME

Who can see the green earth any more
As she was by the sources of Time?
Who imagines her fields as they lay
In the sunshine, unworn by the plough?
Who thinks as they thought,
The tribes who then roam'd on her breast,
Her vigorous primitive sons?

From *The Future* by Matthew Arnold

Imagine the muddy bank of a river that has been hiked along by some ramblers looking for a place to cross. There would be many footprints visible and here and there one might see a sweet paper or an empty soft drink can that had been either accidentally or deliberately dropped. Yet the footprints would greatly outnumber such pieces of litter, and they would clearly mark the route of the walkers even if nothing had been dropped by them.

And footprints, like the people and the animals that make them, can become fossilized. Indeed, many fossil footprints have been discovered, and the scientists who study them are called ichnologists. But although the mud in which footprints are left has to dry out and harden before they can be preserved beneath later sediments as fossils, the muddy banks of every ancient river and stream and water-hole (like those today) acquired numerous footprints daily throughout the whole of their existence, which is why the likelihood of an animal's footprints becoming fossilized is very much greater than the dead animal itself.

Hence if small manufactured objects are occasionally, as the last chapter revealed, found encased in rock, then we can reasonably expect rocks also to bear or contain the fossil footprints of people who have undergone 'whole body' time-slips into the distant past. And because many more of their footprints would be left in ancient mud than lost articles, we would expect fossil human footprints to greatly outnumber rock-bound manufactured items.

And this is what we find. Indeed, the presence of human footprints in rocks dating back many tens of millions of years before mammalian primates, let alone human beings, evolved is one of the most compelling pieces of evidence pointing to the reality of time-slipping. It tells us, despite our feelings to the contrary, that we are not locked into what we call 'the present', but that we can, when the conditions are somehow right for it to happen, be admitted into unimaginably distant ages, and that it may even be possible, through the use of a now thankfully lost technique or method, to visit and explore not only all our yesterdays, but all our tomorrows too.

The world is surprisingly rich in human footprints impressed in rock. In fact just about every country can show examples, not only of human footprints, but also of supposed marks left in rock by fingers, hands, and genuflecting knees. Most are of normal size, but others are larger, sometimes much larger than normal, and therefore seem to have been made by giants. Many are natural depressions, of course, which happen to resemble human footprints or whatever, and a few are the work of artists, having been deliberately carved into the rock. But some, none the less, are genuine imprints left by human beings, whose fossilized presence is impossible to explain by conventional science, for how could people make impressions that pre-date by many millions of years the evolution of human beings?

Our forbears knew nothing about geological processes or about fossil formation, and the presence of human foot, hand or knee prints in rock could only be explained as a miracle, by assuming that the rock had become temporarily plastic when a saint or other holy person placed his or her foot or other body part on it. For example, in AD 545 Saint Medard, having settled a land dispute between some farmers in Picardy, France, marked the new land boundary with a large stone, on which he is said to have placed his foot, and the rock, becoming soft like hot wax beneath it, thereby received its impression.

The following verse from a poem entitled *Footprints of Jesus* apparently draws its inspiration from the footprint ascribed to Our Lord on the Mount of Olives in Jerusalem:

> *I heard them tell how they had tracked*
> *His footsteps o'er the rocky way,*
> *When over Oliphet He walked*
> *To Bethany at close of day,*
> *And down the very hill-side trod*
> *Where oft had passed the Son of God.*

The print of Christ's left foot in the church of the Ascension on the Mount of Olives marks the spot where, according to popular belief, He rose into heaven. There were originally two footprints, one of each foot, at the site but apparently some dastardly Turks removed the right one and placed it in a mosque. Other footprints reputedly made by Jesus in rock are found in the Pas de Dieu chapel in France; in the churches of St Denis and St Laurent in Rome; and in the Rosenstein hermitage in Bavaria, Germany. St Mary's footprints can also be seen in Bavaria, at the chapel of Wurzburg, although it is difficult to understand when, how, or indeed, why Jesus and Mary went to what would have been, in their day, such remote and inhospitable places. Similarly a remarkably well-defined footprint in a stone in the church of St Radegund at Poitiers, France, traditionally marks the place where Christ appeared to St Radegund (AD 518-587), once the wife of the Frankish king Clothaire V, who was initiated into holy orders by the above-mentioned St Medard, then bishop of Noyon. There also appears, on a rock in Champagne, France, a footprint said to be that of St Julian (died AD 117), bishop of Le Mans, to whom modern racing drivers pray. And there are also the supposed foot or knee prints of St Theocrita found on a rock in the Mediterranean island of Paros, and those of St Hyacinth (AD 1185-1257) beside the Garisten river in Poland.

Footmarks ascribed to the Buddha occur on rocks throughout the Far East. The most famous is known as the

Sripada, and stands on the summit of Mount Samanala or Adam's Peak, near Colombo in western Sri Lanka, where the Buddha is believed to have ascended into heaven. But other faiths, however, claim a different origin for this giant footprint. The Moslems, for example, say it was left by Adam, the first man, and marks the spot where he was shown all the ills of the world by an angel. Christians believe it to be the footprint of St Thomas, the apostle who doubted that Jesus had risen from the dead, and who may subsequently have preached the gospel in India, possibly even in Sri Lanka, whereas pious Hindus believe it was left behind by the god Siva. Footprints ascribed to the Buddha also occur on Mount Phrabat in Thailand, on a rock at Nagarahara in India, on a stone at the village of Henzadah in Burma, at several sites in Laos, and in Japan, which is home to seven 'authentic' footprints of the Enlightened One, the most famous of which is found, rather oddly, in Yakushiji cathedral.

The most remarkable British example of footprints in rock are the pair impressed in the rounded top of the Ladykirk stone, found in the church of St Mary at Burwick, South Ronaldsay, in the Orkneys. According to legend, the footprints were left when a man named Gallus (or alternatively, St Magnus) was saved from drowning and carried ashore by a dolphin or a seal, on whose back he had stood, and which was subsequently turned to stone. This fanciful tale was clearly created to explain the presence of the footprints in the curiously rounded upper surface of the rock. But while the footprints are impressive, the rock in which they appear is a type of granite known as a grey whin, which is a dark coloured and very hard igneous rock. This makes it doubly difficult to explain how they got there, if they are genuine, because an igneous rock would only have been soft enough to receive foot impressions when it was molten, although it could not then retain them. And of course an expanse of molten rock would immediately destroy any time-shifter who happened to alight on it. The unshod prints in the Ladykirk stone are 10 inches long and three and a half inches wide.

Similarly, a slab of gneiss known as St Columbkille's

stone, which also bore a pair of footprints, was once on view in Templemore parish, county Derry, Ireland. The footprints were reputed to have been made by the eponymous saint, who is alternatively known as Columba ('the dove', c. AD 521-597), although his identification with them probably only arose after he had consecrated what had originally been a pagan artefact, and which he no doubt did sometime before AD 563, when he left Ireland. However, St Columbkille is credited with the performance of numerous miracles, and he is most famous today for having had the first recorded encounter with the Loch Ness monster, which he repelled with the sign of the cross. But unfortunately, nobody today knows what happened to St Columbkille's Stone, or even if it still exists.

Equally fascinating is the so-called 'devil's footprint' found on the side of a lump of hard, grey igneous rock located just outside the gate of St Mary's church, in Newington, Kent. When I travelled there to view it, I was kindly shown both the footprint and the interesting interior of the church by the Reverend Margaret Mascall. The 'devil's footprint' is not, as we might perhaps expect, the impression of a cloven hoof, but rather is a clearly recognisable human foot, which, unlike the unshod pair impressed in both the Ladykirk stone and St Columbkille's stone, is wearing a shoe. The foot is very large, having a length of fifteen and a half inches and a width across the sole of five inches; this indicates that it was made by someone of gigantic stature, who perhaps stood about eight feet tall. The footprint is made doubly intriguing by the fact that instead of being an impression, it is somewhat outstanding from the rock surface. This suggests to me that it may have been formed when molten rock spread over the surface of a rock that already bore a fossilized foot impression, into which it flowed and thus made a cast of when it hardened, much as the interior of hollow objects can be reproduced inside out by using plaster of Paris. If so, the footprint is necessarily much older than the rock on which it appears, and probably has an age of many tens, if not hundreds, of millions of years.

According to the Reverend William Reeves, there is also

a patch of rock bearing the faint outline of a shod footprint in a church founded by St Patrick at Schirich, in the parish of Skerry, Ireland. The rock is situated close to the north-east angle of the church, and the footprint it bears was formerly an object of great veneration, being ascribed by tradition to St Patrick himself. But it is more likely that the church was built around the footprint, which would have long been regarded as a marvel. However, as I have not been able to view the print for myself, I do not know the type of rock in which it occurs. The Reverend Reeves said that the church stands on a basaltic hill, which may mean that the rock in question is made of basalt. As basalt, like grey whin, is an igneous rock, it adds another dimension to the mystery, as I indicated above.

These and other British/Irish stones bearing footprints were formerly used in Celtic inauguration ceremonies, as Edmund Spencer describes in his *View of the Present State of Ireland*:

> They used to place him that shall be their Captain upon a stone always reserved for that purpose, and placed commonly upon a hill: in many of the which I have seen the foot of a man formed and engraved, which they say was the measure of their first Captain's foot, whereon he standing receives an oath to preserve all the former ancient customs of the country inviolable, and deliver up the succession peaceably to his Tanist, and then had a wand delivered unto him by some whose proper place that is; after which, descending from the stone, he turns himself round about, thrice forward, and thrice backward. (Spelling modernised).

Footprints in rock are by far the most common of such impressions, which is surprising as most people regard their handprints as being more individual to, and more representative of, themselves. Hence on this basis we would expect handprints to outnumber footprints if these remnants had been carved in the rocks, whereas footprints would obviously predominate if they were formed spontaneously, either by a genuine miracle or through a time-slip. Yet a miraculous origin is doubtful in most cases, because the stones bearing the impressions were often known about and venerated long before the arrival of the saint or holy man who became credited with their miraculous formation. In fact such footprints were originally regarded as so special and remarkable, that they were originally thought to have been made by the gods.

Most footprints are found in sedimentary rocks, which is where we would expect them to be if they are real fossil imprints, as indeed most seem to be. Their size varies, although the feet that made most of them would fit comfortably into a pair of modern size 10 or 11 shoes. Hence they were left by people of between 5 feet 9 inches and six feet in height. Others, however, were made by men or perhaps by women of much larger stature. Some are the impressions of shod feet, although most were made by feet that were bare. And while some occur in rocks formed within the last 200,000 years, which means they could have been left by our human ancestors, the majority occur in rocks that are millions of years, sometimes tens or even hundreds of millions of years old, and which therefore precede the evolution of hominids by an impossibly wide margin.

In 1822 the *American Journal of Science* carried a paper by Henry Rowe Schoolcraft (1793-1864) describing the imprints of a pair of human feet, placed side by side, in a slab of limestone rock that had been quarried on a bank of the Mississippi river, near St Louis, Missouri. The 8 foot long, 3.5 foot wide and 8 inches thick slab remained at the quarry for some six years after its discovery, where it attracted great interest, but was then bought by a Mr George Rappe, who soon removed it to his home at Harmony, in Posy county, Indiana, where Henry Schoolcraft, who was both an ethnologist and a geologist, examined it. He wrote of the footmarks:

> The prints are those of a man standing erect, with his heels drawn in, and his toes turned outwards, which is the most natural position. The distance between the

heels, by accurate measurement, is 6 ¼ inches, and between the toes, 13 ½ inches; but it will be perceived, that these are not the impressions of feet accustomed to a close shoe, the toes being very much spread, and the foot flattened in a manner that happens to those who have been habituated to go a great length of time without shoes. Notwithstanding this circumstance, the prints are strikingly natural, exhibiting every muscular impression, the swell of the heel and toes, with a precision and faithfulness to nature, which I have not been able to copy, with perfect exactness, in the present drawing. The length of each foot, as indicated by the prints, is 10 ½ inches, and the width across the spread of the toes, 4 inches, which diminishes to 2 ½ inches, at the swell of the heels, indicating, as it is thought, a stature of the common size.

Henry Schoolcraft remarks of the rock in which these remarkable impressions appear:

'This limestone possesses a firm and compact structure, of the peculiar greyish blue tint common to the calcareous rocks of the Mississippi valley, and contains fossil encrinites, and some analogous remains, very plentifully embedded. It is quarried at St Louis, both for the purposes of building stone, and for quicklime.'

Chalk and limestone rocks were laid down, as I mentioned earlier, during the Cretaceous period, which lasted from about 146 million years to 65 million years ago. The limestone quarried near St Louis is of the floetz type and is formed from foraminifera and the other organisms which lived in the shallow sea that divided the American continent during Late Cretaceous times. It therefore has an age of about 80 million years. Henry Schoolcraft further comments on the limestone slab:

This rock presents a plain and smooth surface, having acquired a polish from the sand and water, to which its original position periodically subjected it. Upon this smooth surface, commencing in front of the tracks, there is a kind of scroll, which is two feet and a

126

half in length. The shape of this is very irregular, and not equally plain and perfect in all parts, and would convey to the observer the idea of man idly marking with his fingers, or with a smooth stick, fanciful figures upon a soft surface.

The man who made the footprints presumably stood either upon a beach or perhaps on one of the many low islands in a lagoon of the shallow Late Cretaceous sea, some 80 million years before our time. The soft ooze was then exposed long enough to the sun and to the air for it to dry out and harden, thereby enabling the footprints to be preserved. However, Henry Schoolcraft mentions the opinion held by a Colonel Benton (presumably Thomas Hart Benton, 1782-1858), and which is certainly pertinent, that because there is no sign of any tracks leading up to or away from the footprints, -- which there ought to have been, for how else did the man get there? -- they cannot be genuine fossils but must have been carved in the rock.

We would certainly expect to see such accompanying tracks if the man belonged to that distant time, and until now it has been a major stumbling block to accepting the footprints as the real thing, even though, as Henry Schoolcraft says:

> The strikingly natural appearance of these prints, has always appeared to me, to be one of the best evidences of their being genuine; for I cannot suppose that there is any artist now in America possessed of the skill necessary to produce such perfect and masterly pieces of sculpture . . . For, let it be constantly be borne in mind, that the antiquity of these prints can be traced back to the earliest discovery of the country, and consequently to the introduction of iron tools and weapons among the aborigines. There are none of our Indian tribes who have made any proficiency in sculpture, even since the iron hatchet and knife, have been exchanged for those of flint, and of obsidian. All their attempts in this way are grotesque, and exhibit a lamentable want of proportions . . .

This seemingly insurmountable difficulty, none the less, can be explained by supposing that the man in question was temporarily time-slipped from the North American Mid-West of relatively modern times, into a day that existed at the same place 80 million years earlier. He was presumably a bare-footed early American Indian, holding a staff or spear, who perhaps had been watching a herd of buffalo, when suddenly, much to his surprise, he found himself standing in another landscape and gazing at a blue sea. Anyone undergoing such an extraordinary translocation would be paralysed with astonishment for several seconds or longer, and he would have gazed dumbfounded around him, trying to comprehend what had happened to him. He may even have scratched an irregular figure (the 'scroll') in the soft ground in front of him with his staff, an unconscious movement caused by fear or apprehension. And if he was then equally quickly time-slipped back to where he came from, the scene he witnessed 80 million years before would appear like a vision, perhaps of some other-worldly paradise. Yet his brief entry into the ancient scene would account for his single pair of footprints, which were afterwards, and equally remarkably, preserved as fossils for examination in relatively recent times.

In a note to his paper, Henry Schoolcraft mentions that two other 'supposed tracks of the human foot' were also discovered impressed in floetz limestone, in 1817, by workmen at a quarry near Herculaneum, in Jefferson county, Missouri, which lies about 30 miles from St Louis. The rock was being extracted to build a stone chimney for a local resident named John W. Honey, but at his direction the two blocks bearing the impressions were incorporated into it, 'in the outside wall, so as to be capable of being examined at all times.' Henry Schoolcraft makes the following comment about them:

> The above arrangement, while it completely preserves, at the same time exposes the prints to observation, in the most satisfactory manner. I

examined them in that position on my first visit to Missouri, in 1818, and afterwards in 1822, when I took drawings of both the prints. They are however the impressions of feet covered with the Indian shoe, and are not so perfect and exquisitely natural as those at Harmony.

It is not clear from Schoolcraft's note if the impressions were of two feet standing at one spot, as in the first case, or if there were instead several footsteps of the same person. Yet what makes them doubly interesting is that the feet of whoever left them were shod, apparently with moccasins or Indian shoes.

They are not the only example of fossil footprints of moccasin-wearing feet. Three other such imprints were discovered in the surface of an expanse of white magnesium limestone on a hillside near the confluence of the Little Cheyenne River with the Cheyenne River, in South Dakota, USA, in 1882 (although they had been known to the local Indians for many years). The smaller size of the footprints indicated that they either belonged to a woman or to an adolescent, and the length of the stride, which was 4 ½ feet between the first two prints and 5 ½ feet between the middle and last, showed that the person who left them had been running. This was confirmed by the greater depth of the heel (at one inch) than the ball of the foot (at half an inch). As the weathered limestone was laid down about 100 million years ago, in the age of the dinosaurs, the person concerned, who must have been time-slipped back to that distant period, may have been fleeing in terror from some hungry reptilian carnivore which had hoped to make a meal of him or her.

Equally astonishing are the two bare, normal-sized human footprints that were found in a bed of carboniferous sandstone in the Cumberland Mountains, of Jackson County, Kentucky at roughly the same date. The sandstone was laid down about 300 million years ago, when amphibians were the dominant vertebrates and when the great coal forests covered the landscape. We can only hope that this American aborigine was time-slipped back to his own era before he disappeared down a carnivorous amphibian's gullet.

These discoveries reveal that several native Americans,

perhaps separated from one another by many tens of years or even longer in the more recent world, underwent almost unbelievably long backward time-slips, although as I have remarked before, it is apparently no more difficult to be time-slipped back 500 million years than it is to be regressed by five days or even five minutes. Moreover, if we take into account a) the small chance of such footsteps being preserved as fossils, and b) of them ever being found, it suggests that many North American Indians have been time-slipped back, perhaps spontaneously, into the distant past, a conclusion that applies equally to other peoples around the world, and which in turn reveals that time-slipping is a far commoner bizarre occurrence than anyone could have imagined.

Then, in June 1968, an amateur fossil collector named William J. Meister found, at Antelope Spring, Utah, what are probably the oldest and certainly the most incredible fossil footprints of all, which were made by the feet of someone wearing sandals or flip-flops.

Meister was out with a group of fellow enthusiasts looking for fossil trilobites in the ancient shale formations of the area, when he quite by chance picked up and split open, with his geological hammer, a two-inch thick piece of shale. The rock broke neatly apart to reveal 'on one side the footprint of a human being with trilobites right in the footprint itself'. The other half of the rock slab showed an almost perfect mould of the footprint and fossils. Amazingly the human was wearing a sandal!

Trilobites were highly successful crawling marine invertebrates, somewhat resembling large woodlice, and they dominated the seas during the Cambrian period, which began about 600 million years ago and ended one hundred million years later. They subsequently underwent something of an evolutionary eclipse, but managed to survive, although in dwindling numbers, until the middle of the Permian period, about 250 million years ago, when they became extinct. The sandaled human foot that helped speed up this process was 10 ¼ inches long and 3 ½ inches wide, so indicating that it belonged to a man of about 5 feet 9 inches in height. His incredible time-slip took him back about 500 million years, when he suddenly found himself on that late Cambrian beach. We can only guess at the astonished thoughts that must have raced through his mind, and wonder if he was left marooned there or if he was equally speedily returned to his own time. Unfortunately no fossilized maker's name is visible on the sandal's sole, yet its rather unstylish shape appears to be that of a cheap import, which indicates that the buyer was not well-off, while his inability to see what he was stepping on suggests that he was perhaps short-sighted. Together, these clues reveal he was probably an ordinary American palaeontologist of the last thirty or so years, who stepped out one summer's day to collect fossil trilobites at Antelope Spring, who passed through that amazing time-slip door which suddenly swung open, and who next found himself treading on the real thing. It might almost be said that he had entered his own paradise.

Then, on 20 July 1968, following William Meister's incredible find, the Antelope Spring fossil site was visited by a professional geologist named Dr Clifford Burdick, from Tucson, Arizona, who quickly discovered in the shale, but at a different place, the impression of a child's bare foot, about six inches long, whose effect upon the originally soft ground showed clear signs that it was contemporaneous with the rock itself.

> 'The rock chanced to fracture along the front of the toes before the fossil footprint was found,' Dr Burdick noted. 'On cross section the fabric of the rock stands out in fine laminations, or bedding planes. Where the toes pressed into the soft material, the laminations were bowed downward from the horizontal, indicating a weight that had been pressed into the mud'.

Such an effect is impossible to fake, and proves beyond doubt that the child, who seemingly had never worn shoes and was thus probably also of American Indian ancestry, was there some 500 million years previously. And that further astounding find is bolstered by the discovery of two prints of feet wearing sandals or possibly shoes, which were found the following month, this time by a Salt Lake City school teacher, but again at a spot apart from the previous two. Hence three individuals, but doubtless more, have on separate occasions been time-slipped from the same place to the same, but earlier place, and there witnessed the wonder (or the horror) of the 'pre-Adamite' world.

But none the less, despite the astounding nature and incredible significance of these fossil human footprints, the most wonderful and conclusive fossil evidence that has ever been discovered was also made at Aix-en-Provence, in France, where, as we noted in the last chapter, petrified tools were discovered in 1783 which closely matched those used by the quarrymen who dug them up. On this other occasion, which took place sixteen years earlier in 1767, the fossil bones of human beings were recovered from a rock that was many tens of millions of years older than the human race!

The quarry where the discovery was made, however, was not the same as the one at Aix which yielded the petrified tools. This is what the *Annual Register* for 1767, which was one publication that reported the find, said about the rock in which the discovery took place:

> A rock, which is there level with the surface of the ground, was sapped by gunpowder; it formed a very hard mass, and no strata were observable in it; the part of this rock, which lay buried in the earth to a certain depth, was covered with a bed of clay, over which was vegetable earth: The interior of the rock was of the nature of the hardest marble, and mingled with jaspared and transparent veins.

I formerly mentioned that limestone strata occur around Aix, that they were laid down in Cretaceous times in the shallow sea which then covered the region, and that they are about one hundred million years old. Marble is a white, fine-grained, hard and smooth rock, much used in the construction of buildings and monuments and for statuary, and is seemingly very different from the much softer, more crumbly and porous limestone. But in fact marble is formed from limestone by a process known as metamorphosis, brought about by both pressure and heat, and thus has an identical chemical composition to limestone. Hence despite the interior of the rock at Aix being described as having the 'nature of the hardest marble' and not being actually marble, it was doubtlessly a variety of metamorphosed limestone and thus at least one hundred million years old. The account continues:

> At a depth (in the rock) of four feet and a half were discovered bodies of a pretty regular figure, and resembling human heads; the occiputs of some of them have been preserved: they were incrusted with the stone, and their internal parts full of it: The face of one of those heads was preserved without alteration; it is in the natural proportions; the eyes, the nose well formed, though flatted, the cheeks, the mouth, the chin, are therein distinguished, and the muscles of the whole very well articulated. This head is of the same substance with the stone it was taken out of. It was after penetrating into it five feet in depth, that a great quantity of bones were discovered to be lodged in it: They were held as having belonged to different parts of the human body; jaw bones, teeth, arm and thigh bones, all were confirmed as such: They had not, in appearance, changed their nature; their cavity was filled with a crystalline substance, or stony matter like to that which enclosed them.

In 1767 it was still generally accepted that the earth and all the rocks in it were created by God in 4004 BC, the year in which He also made Adam, the first man. Because this meant the fossil human bones found at Aix were necessarily more recent, their stunning importance and anomalous nature was not appreciated at the time. They were regarded simply as curiosities, which is apparently why they were not preserved for posterity. But it is evident that if their identification as human fossils is correct -- and there does not seem to have been any doubt about that -- they are perhaps the most important fossils ever discovered. For they either completely overturn all that is known about human evolution, or they are conclusive evidence, as I believe, to the reality of time-shifting.

And uniquely, the amount of human fossil material discovered was dramatically large, especially when we consider that the discovery of one fossil human tooth or a fragment of jawbone can render modern palaeontologists ecstatic. For not only were the complete remains of one individual found, but those of several, which suggests that a group of people died together. We may wonder how this tragedy occurred. It may be that they were a group of inexperienced time-slipping tourists, who started out from that spot when it was dry land and went back further than they should have done. Hence when they materialised in 'the past' they found, to their horror, that it wasn't dry land any more, and they were instead splashing helplessly around in the sea.

And that's why their fossil bones were found mixed with the fossils of fish skeletons!

CHAPTER SEVEN

THE GREAT EXPERIMENT

Long ago Time's mighty billows
Swept your footsteps from the sand.

From *Phantoms* by Adelaide Procter

The very number of fossil human footprints and rock-encased artefacts, as well as the unique discovery of extremely ancient fossil human bones, naturally suggests that not all those who visited 'the past' were the helpless victims of spontaneous time-slips but had actually caused them to happen. Some may even have been time-slipping tourists, for once an escape can be effected from what we call 'the present', visiting 'the past' would be an impossible to resist temptation, although one not without its dangers. And 'the future' would be equally alluring if it can be entered in the same or a similar way.

Indeed, time-slipping may provide the answer to one of the last great mysteries of archaeology, which is how and why did the sudden and unexpected growth of civilised city life alongside the Nile, the Tigris and Euphrates, the Indus and other rivers, take place? Such river valleys had been populated for millennia by Neolithic hunter-gatherers, who enjoyed stable, traditional, tribal lives. Yet during an incredibly brief period lasting from one to two centuries that was all to change. Almost overnight rude villages grew into walled towns; and agriculture, irrigation, the use of metal for tools and weapons, and writing and numeracy, became relatively commonplace; governance by kings and the rule of law happened; and the concept of gods in human form took root. These periods of rapid development began at least as early as the middle of the fourth millennium BC in Egypt and Sumer, yet later elsewhere.

The immensity of these changes is without parallel in the history of the human race. The Neolithic people living beside the Euphrates river, for example, dwelt in huts built of mud and reeds. So how could they suddenly not only master the art of baking bricks, but eventually design and construct large cities containing grandiose palaces, airy houses and store rooms, delightful gardens, and echoing temples with them? From where did they obtain the knowledge of building techniques, brick strength, mathematics, drainage, and architectural design that such construction would require? And how did they learn about all the dozens of other complex skills and jobs that they enthusiastically adopted at the same time? Their astounding transformation from simple rustic hunter-gatherers into much more sophisticated town dwellers, which was repeated in Egypt and in other parts of the world, makes our modern-day technological advances seem like mere sleight of hand.

Fortunately, we know the answer to some of these questions -- or at least we know how those ancient peoples said they received such important and transmogrifying knowledge: it was given to them, so they claimed, by the gods. And to impart the numerous skills, crafts, techniques, and methods to them, the gods came and lived amongst them for many years, often becoming their first kings, which thereby enabled the gods to organise them into an urban society, and then, once their civilising mission was completed, they left and never returned.

This arrival and subsequent departure of the gods, which is recorded in the so-called myths and legends of the peoples concerned, has led some writers, following the lead set by Erich von Daniken, to postulate that 'the gods' were actually visitors from outer space. But while this was an intriguing hypothesis which once captured the popular imagination, it is almost certainly wrong.

For according to the ancient texts, the gods, if we may call them that for the moment, were human in shape and form, spoke the language of the people they visited, were both mortal and vulnerable to human diseases, and neither arrived nor departed in spaceships. And while their knowledge was impressive compared to that of the Neolithic tribal groups amongst whom they came to live, it was not particularly technologically advanced. Indeed, they appear to have come from societies that were in many ways not a great deal further developed than those they brought into being.

This necessarily means they were not extra-terrestrials. And neither were they gods, although they would have seemed like deities to the illiterate, semi-barbaric, animal and storm-worshipping people to whom they brought their benefits. We have a modern parallel to the profound effect engendered on the indigenous natives, in the cargo cults of the Pacific islands, which developed when Westerners who took supplies to the islands during and after the Second World War became transformed, on their departure, into beneficent deities by the locals, and whose return is still desired and prayed for today.

Where then did those more knowledgeable people come from? They might have originated from some neighbouring region which had simply evolved faster. But if civilisation had arisen elsewhere, it would not only have left behind extensive ruins and artefacts, which have not been found, but it would have impinged upon surrounding areas and significantly altered their development. There is, however, no evidence for this. And language difficulties would have prevented advanced incomers from a distant place, who did not arrive as conquerors, from being able to pass on their knowledge and skills. We must also remember that ancient societies did not send out volunteers to teach the delights of civilisation to the socially disadvantaged; they simply were not altruistic in that way.

But if 'time travel' is possible, such people could have come from 'the future', from a date some two hundred or more years ahead of their time of arrival; and by their speaking the same language, it suggests that they belonged to the same racial group, which would necessarily have developed more slowly had they not, by their actions, speeded things up. These time-shifters therefore went back because they discovered how to do so, and they did it, not out of altruism, but instead to benefit their own society. It was, however, a misguided endeavour, and it went disastrously wrong. We are still paying a heavy price for it.

Yet before discussing further what those time-shifters were hoping to achieve, we must first look at some of the old legends which describe them and at the poisoned chalice of benefits they brought. We will examine their arrival in, and their departure from Egypt, Sumer, Italy, Etruria, Greece, Mexico, and South America. Their activities are most fully described by the ancient Egyptian scribes, but the changes they brought about elsewhere were generally the same. The Egyptian experiment was one of the earliest, but it was not the first, which happened in Sumer, in modern Iraq.

The Egyptian records state that there were nine original gods or divine pharaohs, who came and lived in Egypt and who taught its Neolithic inhabitants about civilised life. This Ennead or group of nine consisted of one original time-shifter from whom the rest are descended, although all probably returned to and from their own time at intervals and also permanently in old age. Several of the nine are unique among the many dozens of Egyptian gods in being represented in statues, wall carvings, and paintings as human in form, in contrast to the half-human, half-animal portrayals of the rest. This also suggests, as many ancient historians say, that they were really human beings who were later deified. However, those that are shown as part animal may actually have developed physical deformities due to in-breeding.

At Memphis, the capital of Upper Egypt, the first divine pharaoh was named Ptah, while at Heliopolis, the capital of Lower Egypt, he was called Ra or Re. It is possible that two different people are referred to, yet because both Ptah and Ra are said to father the other 'gods', they are probably identical. The different names therefore probably reflect the intense rivalry that later grew up between Memphis and Heliopolis.

Ptah is described as being a fair-skinned, clean-shaven individual, and is always shown wearing a close-fitting hat, which covers the nape of his neck, and which thus resembles both a modern swimming hat and a First World War leather flying helmet. Indeed, his curious stream-lined head wear and his equally unusual tight-fitting robe, which archaeologists say is a funerary winding sheet, give Ptah a decidedly contemporary appearance. He is additionally usually portrayed standing with his arms extended outwards from his robe, and holding in one of his hands a rod or sceptre, which later became a symbol of both divinity and kingship, although it was probably, as we shall see, a weapon of considerable power brought by him from 'the future'.

Ptah is credited with introducing into Neolithic Egypt metal-working, building, and artistic design, which is why he later became a patron of both artists and artisans, while through his creation of the other gods, says Professor John A. Wilson, there 'came into being all of the divine order; thus were made the directive destinies which supplied mankind with food and provisions; thus was made the distinction between right and wrong; thus were made all arts, crafts, and human activities; thus Ptah made provinces and cities and set the various local gods in their governing places.' Hence Ptah was responsible for the initial establishment of Egyptian civilisation.

According to the legends of Heliopolis, however, the first divine pharaoh was Ra, who not only taught the people practical skills like those attributed to Ptah, but who divided Egypt into twelve provinces. Additionally, Ra possessed a formidable weapon called a Uraeus, which is described as a sacred asp that spat fire, and which he kept concealed, for everyone's safety, in a golden box. When necessary, the Uraeus was used to defeat those who took up arms against him. As we shall see, the rod of Ptah and Ra's Uraeus may have been two versions of the same device. Even more remarkably, the Uraeus and its golden box closely resemble the equally destructive Ark of the Covenant made by the Hebrews following Jehovah's instructions.

It is said that Ra ruled Egypt in a just and peaceful way for a great many years, and like any real person (but unlike a god) he gradually grew old and decrepit. Yet he remained pharaoh until his grand-daughter, Isis, tricked him into revealing his secret name, whereupon he vanished into the sky and became the sun-god. This may mean that when he disappeared he returned to 'the future', and that his 'secret name' was in fact a word or sound which, when uttered, brought about the necessary time-slip.

Equally interesting is the fact that Ra had two twin children, a son named Shu and a daughter named Tefnut, of whose generation by Ra the Pyramid Texts says 'Thou didst spit what was Shu; thou didst splutter out what was Tefnut', which may mean that they were born by Ra's wife in his 'own time' and that he had to utter a difficult to enunciate word to prompt their time-slip move from there. Then, after their arrival, Shu and Tefnut rather surprisingly marry one another, although it has not been explained why they entered into this incestuous union, when they could easily have found spouses in the wider Egyptian population. Such incest only makes sense if the pair were strictly forbidden from having sexual relationships with the people of that time, as this would have had, or so it was presumably feared by Ra, unknown and unpredictable future consequences, which might even have precluded them from being born. Hence incest between Shu and Tefnut was preferable to outside marriages which might have produced such dire consequences. The young married couple then, in turn, had two twin children, a son, whom they named Geb, and a daughter, Nut.

Egypt is a hot, dry country, and most of it is barren desert. Agriculture is only possible beside the Nile or in its delta. The river floods regularly in July, when it deposits vast quantities of fertile alluvial silt beside itself; and the water does not fully subside until late October or November, when the crops are sown.

Shu and Tefnut's contribution towards improving the lives of the native Nile dwellers seems to have centred on teaching them how to utilize the land more efficiently. They showed them how to increase the amount of land suitable for agriculture by cutting down and removing the extensive beds of reeds and other vegetation growing in the Nile delta and along the banks of the river; then how to retain the water in such defoliated areas by building earth walls around them; then how to pump water into the higher enclaves when the flooding was unusually low, as sometimes happens; and lastly how to cut irrigation canals.

In myth, the Nile is said to be the home of a great serpent named Apep, which symbolizes the sinuous, difficult to control river. Shu's management of the Nile thus came to be pictured as him fighting with Apep's children, which are the various tributaries, streams, bays, reed beds and so on, as well as the original inhabitants of their banks, who were most affected by his activities. The myth also relates how the children of Apep attacked Shu in his palace at Nub, although he overcame them after a desperate fight. However, not long afterwards Shu fell sick from a dreadful disease, whose disfiguring effects prompted his followers to rebel against him. This illness further affirms Shu's humanity and mortality, and was probably a water-borne ailment, perhaps amoebic dysentery, that he contracted from the Nile. When the disease proved untreatable, and following a violent storm that lasted for nine days, Shu vacated his throne in favour of his son Geb, and afterwards presumably returned for medical assistance to his own time, as it is recounted that he vanished into the air.

Both Shu and Tefnut were later deified, Shu becoming the god of the air, and Tefnut the goddess of the dew and the rain. Like Ptah and Ra, Shu and Tefnut are always represented in human form.

During Shu's rule Geb likewise married his twin sister Nut, albeit secretly. But while this union happened for the reasons given above, it was evidently not wholly accepted by Shu, who, it is said, actually once pulled the pair apart while they were copulating. Geb also made the mistake, early in his reign, of opening the golden box containing Ra's Uraeus, which spat out fire and killed his companions and badly burned him. Fortunately, however, the box, it is said, also contained Ptah's rod or cane and a lock of his hair, and it was with the latter that his burns were healed. Geb subsequently became a wise and responsible ruler, whose great contribution towards the civilisation of Egypt was the carrying out of a detailed survey of the country.

At first, Geb's wife Nut had difficulty in conceiving a

child, which was perhaps caused by her genetic closeness to her brother/husband, although she eventually gave birth to three sons, respectively named Osiris (or Ousir), Thoth (or Thaut), and Set (or Seth), and two daughters, named Isis and Nephthys, making a total of five offspring. Then after Geb and Nut 'ascended into heaven' or returned, in other words, to their own time, they were deified by the later Egyptians, Geb becoming the god of the earth and Nut the goddess of the sky. This conveniently allowed their father's forcible separation of them while love-making to be represented as the separation of the earth and sky in order to create the world.

The work done by Ra, Shu and Geb, and Shu and Geb's spouses, to introduce (or to update) agriculture, flood control and irrigation, building, metal-work, the manufacture of tools and so on, did not proceed without resistance. The Neolithic hunter-gatherers of the area were not keen to change their traditional ways, and much persuasion, exhortation and even force were needed to convince them to do so. We must also remember that despite their later deification, the five time-shifters were not gods and had no divine powers, and neither were they at that time absolute rulers; and apart from the Uraeus and its copies, which were used only against the armed and violent, all they possessed was a greater knowledge of agricultural methods and the other skills and arts they introduced, and of the social benefits that these would bring.

The increasing use of agriculture in Egypt and the growth of what we may properly call civilisation accompanying this, happened during the reign of the fourth divine pharaoh, Osiris. He was born at Thebes, which was then a village, and he grew to be a tall, handsome, bearded, and dark-skinned man, who was by nature gentle and persuasive. He is typically represented in art as holding both a shepherd's crook and a whip, the first signifying his loving role as a guide and shepherd of the people, the second his determination to get things done.

One of Osiris's first tasks as a civiliser was to eradicate cannibalism, which was still practiced in the more remote country districts, the next to carry on the work of Shu by teaching his subjects how to prepare the cleared and drained land and grow crops on it, and how to make and use efficient agricultural implements like the hoe, the adze, and the plough, with flint or copper blades, and wooden flails for threshing corn. Equally important was his introduction of a new type of wheat known as emmer (*Triticum dioccum*), which is superior to dinkel and the other wild grasses that had previously been harvested. Indeed, emmer produces a better tasting grain and has a higher yield. He also introduced the growing of hops and grapes, and subsequently taught the arts of brewing beer and fermenting wine. Taken together, these changes improved, increased, and regulated the food supply and so promoted population growth and settled communities; they also created a food surplus that could be stored in granaries as security against crop failure, and which in turn freed many individuals from agricultural production, so allowing them to acquire the new skills he taught and to take up different occupations.

Osiris is likewise credited with founding the organised state religion, which subsequently became very important in Egypt. The indigenous Neolithic hunter-gatherers believed in a variety of spirits, totems and nature gods, and Osiris made use of their superstitious fears by encouraging them to worship his own forebears, whom they already regarded as gods. This highly important and deliberate act happened alongside the building of temples and the introduction of temple worship, both previously unknown, and also the representation of 'the gods' in magnificent stone images, etc., which heightened and thus helped sustain belief. By turning his family into gods, Osiris anthropomorphized religion, which as we shall see happened in a similar way elsewhere, and ensured that the time-shifters and the civilisation they brought would be maintained. Osiris also enacted just laws which enabled the growing urban populations to live peaceably together. It was for these reasons he earned the laudatory title of Onnophris, meaning 'The Good One'.

Like Shu and Geb before him, Osiris married one of his sisters, namely Isis. She was not, however, his twin, but

The "Goddess" Isis

rather the (identical) twin of her sister Nephthys. Nephthys
in turn married their brother Set. Isis worked closely with
Osiris, and she is said to have introduced corn grinding and
bread baking, and spinning and weaving, to the women of
Egypt. She further encouraged domestic life by instituting
marriage and by codifying the duties and responsibilities of
both husband and wife. Additionally, Isis taught those men
who had once been farmers how to cure the sick and
wounded. They thereby became the first Egyptian doctors.

The growth of settled village and town life happened
fastest in the Nile delta, where the population was largest and
more accessible. In time the agricultural innovations and the
greater control and efficiency of farming they brought
gradually spread up the river, which made it increasingly
difficult for Osiris to supervise what was happening there. He

had also been fired with an ambition to leave Egypt, albeit temporarily, and bring civilisation to other parts of the Middle East. He therefore divided the country into two administrative areas, each of which contained a number of provinces; the first, which comprised the delta, came to be known as Lower Egypt, whose capital was Heliopolis, over which he retained control, while the river itself, which ran through the hot and barren desert, was called Upper Egypt, whose capital was at Memphis, and was given in charge of his brother Set. That done, he left behind his beautiful Queen as regent of Lower Egypt, and set off on his self-appointed civilising mission accompanied by his grand vizier and brother Thoth and a number of helpers.

Unfortunately the stage was now set for an inter-familial tragedy, which partly stemmed from the amount of in-breeding that had gone on, creating as it did mental and physical problems, and partly from the ever-growing jealousy felt by Set towards Osiris. For Set, the youngest of the three sons, had neither the charm, sophistication or talent of Osiris, nor his good looks. He was in fact a typical gauche and churlish, yet wild and rough, younger brother, who was remarkable only for his red hair and pale skin. And notwithstanding the importance of the task he had been given, which was to civilise the primitive peoples of the Upper Nile, Set considered that he had been shunted off into a backwater by Osiris. His angry and resentful feelings deepened as reports from the outside regions visited by Osiris told him how successful his brother's civilising mission was. And to make matters worse, Set was unable to father a son, or indeed any child, on his wife Nephthys, and she deepened his sense of inadequacy by constantly comparing him unfavourably with Osiris.

When Osiris returned to Egypt many months later he was welcomed by all, with the exception of Set and his cronies, and there were wild and raucous celebrations, enlivened by the drinking of alcohol, throughout the land of Egypt. Osiris and Isis spent long nights locked in one another's embrace, which did not please Nephthys, who was secretly in love with Osiris and who wanted nothing more than to change places with her twin. But it was not until Isis happily revealed that she was pregnant by Osiris, which was like a cruel stab in the heart to Nephthys, that she resolved to act on her desires.

Nephthys's opportunity came one evening when Isis happened to be engaged elsewhere. The love-sick twin made Osiris drunk, pulled him into her arms, and Osiris, befuddled into thinking he was with Isis, made passionate love to her. And afterwards, when Osiris fell into a deep sleep, Nephthys slid herself out from underneath him and retired to her quarters, overjoyed that she carried his semen within her. But her treachery had not gone unobserved, for Set had followed her secretly to Osiris's room and had waited until she left it breathless and red-faced, which told him that he had been cuckolded. And when he eventually discovered that Nephthys was pregnant his anger and jealousy towards Osiris boiled over. Unknowingly, the beloved Osiris, now known as 'The Universal Lord' by his adopted people, had signed his own death warrant.

Set murdered Osiris by means of a stratagem. One night at a great feast held at Memphis to celebrate Osiris's return, Set and seventy-two fellow conspirators (for that is the number traditionally given) brought out a beautifully-made chest, which attracted everyone's admiration. With a pleasant laugh, Set told the company that he would give the chest to whoever fitted inside it exactly, and Osiris, falling in with the mood of the moment, volunteered to try it for size. But no sooner had Osiris laid himself down in the chest, than Set and his accomplices closed the lid upon him and nailed it firmly down. Then without heeding Osiris's muffled cries, they carried the chest down to the Nile and threw it in. The swiftly flowing river soon carried it downstream and out of sight.

This evil act happened in the twenty-eighth year of Osiris's reign, and it resulted in Osiris's death by drowning. The chest containing his body was swept out into the Mediterranean and eventually made its way to a beach near the town of Byblos, in Phoenicia. There a tamarisk or, as some say, a sycamore tree, grew up around it and completely enclosed it. Later the tree was cut down and used to make pillars for a temple, which is where Isis, who had spent the intervening time searching for Osiris, recognised the chest as part of one of the pillars. She persuaded Malcandre, the king of Byblos, to let her have the precious relic, and she secretly returned with it to the town of Buto in Lower Egypt.

Set, meanwhile, had made himself lord of all Egypt, and those members of his family that refused to recognize his overlordship, who included Thoth and his own wife Nephthys, then heavily pregnant with Osiris's child, had to hide themselves from his wrath amid the swamps of the Nile delta. And still angry with his brother, Set deliberately failed to support or encourage the agricultural innovations that Osiris had introduced, by allowing the peasants to drift away from the newly cultivated land and to return to their previous shiftless lifestyles. In many areas this neglect led to a renewed growth of the desert, which is why Set later became deified as the god of the desert. Legend says that Set was Egypt's divine pharaoh for two hundred years, which is possible if he returned to 'the future' and only came back at intervals, but it is doubtful that his position was sufficiently secure to permit such long absences. Hence in truth his reign probably only lasted two hundred lunar months, which is about sixteen and a half years.

Isis meanwhile, following her return to Buto, went into hiding along with her family and followers in the swampy Nile delta, taking the uncorrupted body of her husband with her. But Set was in the habit of hunting at night in the swamps, where he quite by chance came across the spot where the coffin containing Osiris's body lay. He immediately removed the corpse, took it gleefully away with him and, to prevent any future resuscitation attempt on it, hacked it into fourteen pieces, which, it is said, he scattered promiscuously around the land of Egypt.

Isis was devastated when she discovered the theft, but her mood turned to one of outrage when she learned what Set had done to her beloved's body. She immediately set out to find his remains, and spent many months journeying tirelessly throughout Egypt looking for them. She was successful in locating thirteen of the dismembered pieces, but failed to find Osiris's penis, which had apparently been left by Set, in a final act of revenge, at a place inhabited by an oxyrhynchus crab, which ate it.

During Isis's absence, her twin sister Nephthys gave birth to a son, Osiris's child, whom she named Anubis. In most representations of Anubis in wall paintings and sculptures, he is shown with the body of a man and the head of a jackal, which is why he eventually became the jackal god. This strange development may reflect an actual deformity of Anubis's head resulting from the incestuous in-breeding of his family. Similarly, Isis's child, a prematurely born son, apparently had the head of (or one similar to) a falcon. She called the boy Hor-sa-iset, but he is better known to us as Horus.

On her return to Egypt with the thirteen surviving parts of Osiris's body, Isis put them carefully together and, with the help of Nephthys, Horus, her little nephew Anubis, and her brother Thoth, performed magic ceremonies over them until they not only rejoined one another but returned to life, albeit deficient in one particular. Such incompleteness perhaps explains why Osiris, although delighted to be alive again and with Isis, declined to resume his throne, but instead left the world and, it is said, became the lord of the dead. This may mean that he time-slipped 'back to the future', where he no doubt hoped the more advanced medical and surgical skills available might be sufficient to restore him to full masculinity. And while the story of his murder and dismemberment, his dead body's failure to decay, and his restoration to life, sound completely fantastic, it is possible that if everything described took place within a far shorter period, and if Isis's magic powers were really advanced powers of psychic healing, then Osiris may well have been put back together and resuscitated as described.

The Osiris family group remained in the delta swamps, hiding from Set and his followers, for several years, until Horus, a physically weak child, was big and robust enough to attempt to avenge his father and ascend the throne. In this he was assisted by his resurrected father, who made frequent returns from 'the future' and so instructed him in warfare and the use of arms. Yet Set fiercely resisted Horus's attacks; and the war between the two leaders and their respective armies went on for many years without either gaining the upper hand.

But the war was finally brought to an end when the 'men from the future' or a tribunal of 'gods' -- presumably Ptah/Ra, Shu and Geb -- came to see what was going on. They discovered, to their horror, that Set's mismanagement threatened the entire civilisation project, and thereby gave Horus his birthright, the throne of all Egypt. Set and his associates were punished by being put to death. In later times Set became the personification of evil, and Egyptian mothers would frighten their children into being good by simply mentioning his name. However, the changes and upheavals brought about by the civilisation project were not liked by everyone, and Set had enjoyed widespread support among those who preferred a more easy-going lifestyle and who came to look back at the past with nostalgic regret. Indeed, we have already noted how Shu, the grandfather of Set and Osiris, encountered fierce resistance from those indigenous people who did not want to be civilised.

The new young king resumed Osiris's agricultural and irrigation policies, thereby encouraging a return to the land, and he built new temples, in which he allowed himself to be worshipped. Indeed, Horus and his parents Osiris and Isis were soon regarded as a 'divine' triad, similar to that of Christianity's Father, Son and Holy Ghost. Horus in due course married Hathor, who was later worshipped, among other things, as a sky-goddess. This suggests that she was specifically time-slipped back to become his wife, for Horus did not have a sister to marry. He is further said to have ruled Egypt for three hundred years, which is quite possible if he returned to 'the future' and only returned at intervals, but if we once again interpret this as meaning three hundred lunar months, it gives the more likely period of twenty-four years and eight months. Then Horus, from whom the later pharaohs claimed descent, vacated the throne in favour of his uncle Thoth.

Thoth is perhaps the most interesting of the time-shifters who dedicated themselves to civilising Egypt, and he was able to build on the work of his forebears, who had painstakingly taught the essential arts of agriculture, irrigation, metal-working, brick making and building, pottery, spinning and weaving, and so on, to the savage and cannibal hunter-gatherers who had occupied the Nile valley and delta, so making them increasingly settled, stable, and civilised. Thoth in fact was a genius, who used his wide knowledge and intellectual skills to teach the cleverer peasants, who could be released from farm work by the growing food surpluses, first how to write using hieroglyphics, and then the elements of such varied subjects as astronomy, medicine, surgery, mathematics, geometry, surveying, art and drawing, music composition and musical instrument making, and record keeping and accountancy. Indeed, Thoth impressed upon the Egyptians the importance of recording their own history, as he knew, like T.S. Eliot, that

> *A people without history*
> *Is not redeemed from time, for history is a pattern*
> *Of timeless moments . . .*

. . . and that a shared history would help consolidate the nation. In this way he created an educated elite from which teachers, civil servants, doctors, artists, poets, historians, and other professionals could be drawn, who were needed to run an increasingly complex society and who could generate ideas and inventions.

Thoth was in many ways therefore a wise and enlightened pharaoh, whose long peaceful reign gave civilised life the chance to develop roots and properly to establish itself. And yet, by the greatest irony, it was Thoth who ruined the great experiment, and it was sex that brought it about.

Thoth was unable to marry either of his two sisters, for they had returned to 'the future', and anyhow, Isis was still married to Osiris. But he was a strongly sexed man, and like many clever intellectuals, more than a little stupid where women were concerned. He knew that inbreeding had worryingly produced both deformed children and impaired fertility, and he resolved not only to copy Horus by marrying outside the family, but to increase his chances of having healthy children by taking three wives. Lust may also have played a role in this decision.

However, polygamy was illegal in his own society of 'the future', so in order to keep his actions secret, Thoth took the strictly forbidden and dangerous step of uniting himself with three local women, named Seshat, Nehmuit, and Maat. We know that Seshat and Nehmuit each bore him a son, and he probably also fathered daughters as well. By doing this Thoth introduced into the time equation people who should not have been there, who had indeed not been in 'the past' from which his own society had evolved, and whose descendants would literally change the future and eliminate him and his family. This explains why Thoth is the last 'god' whom tradition clearly states came and lived amongst the people of Egypt, and why none of the other 'gods' were ever seen again.

Eventually Thoth became too old to continue as pharaoh and he retired and returned to 'the future'. Prior to his departure he taught the temple priests how to construct a workable calendar, which was necessary for planning religious rituals and for determining when the Nile would flood. This led to him being called, like the moon, the 'measurer of time', and in later years he became so closely identified with the moon that he was called the Moon god. It also explains why some statues show him with the head of a dog crowned with a crescent moon, for the nocturnal howling of dogs links them with the moon. Thoth's gift of the calendar was remembered by the Egyptian people, who named the first month of year after him.

Exactly who followed Thoth as divine pharaoh is uncertain, due to the patchy and variable extant accounts, but because the work of civilising Egypt was completed under him, we need not follow the course of 'time-shifter' rule any further. We do know, however, that the first local Egyptian pharaoh, who was thus not a time-shifter, was named Hor-aha (or Fighting Hawk), although he is more familiarly known as Menes. He would almost certainly have been a member of the aristocratic ruling class, and could thereby claim descent from 'the gods'. Hor-aha founded the First Dynasty of pharaohs in about 3400 BC. He was responsible for unifying the country, which had become divided into two kingdoms again during the troubled period following Thoth's departure. Indeed, while the great experiment had been a magnificent success for Egypt, it was a disaster for 'the future' from which Ptah and his descendants had come.

What then went wrong? Well, the civilisation project was conducted, as indicated, to hasten the rate of social evolution and to benefit thereby both the future Egypt and the adjacent countries from which the time-shifters originated. Let me help explain this by quoting again from Mark Twain's *A Yankee at the Court of King Arthur*, the novel in which an American from 1873 is spontaneously taken back some thirteen hundred years to sixth century England. During a three year period, the hero of the story, with a dogged persistence, introduces a number of nineteenth century ideas and inventions to that Dark Age society, which resulted in the following changes:

> Now look around on England. A happy and prosperous country, and strangely altered . . . slavery was dead and gone; all men were equal before the law; taxation had been equalised. The telegraph, the telephone, the phonograph, the type-writer, the sewing machine, and all the thousand willing and handy servants of steam and electricity were working their way into favour. We had a steamboat or two on the Thames, we had steam war-ships, and the beginning of a steam commercial marine; I was getting ready to send out an expedition to discover America.

Now if these stupendous changes had taken root in the sixth century and had led to an ensuing explosion of ideas and inventions, then obviously the wonders of twenty-first century science and technology might have come into being by the eighth or the ninth century AD. And if the rate of technological and social development had continued to accelerate, it would have resulted in a very different nineteenth century to that from which Mark Twain's fictional time-slipper came; one in fact that would have been different in every way.

Hence by introducing what were advanced techniques of agriculture, metal working, building and so on, to the Neolithic hunter-gatherers of the Nile valley in the middle of the fourth millennium BC, Ptah and his fellow time-shifters hoped to create civilisation centuries before it would otherwise have evolved (which they did), in order that their society, which lay perhaps two or three centuries in 'the future', would reap the enormous benefits of an earlier start. But it was always a gamble, for they could never completely control the results.

The time-slippers had seemingly hoped that the same people would still be born, who would of course be their ancestors, and they were particularly concerned about the possible negative future effects of their mating with the locals. This suggests that they knew such unions had the potential to wipe them out altogether, by preventing them from being born, which is what seems to have happened. For once Thoth vacates the throne of Egypt the time-shifters or 'gods' no longer appear. Their place is taken by a number of so-called 'demi-gods' who are evidently the descendants of Thoth's union with local women. And the reign of the demi-gods, while apparently long, eventually ends when Menes or Hor-aha seizes power and founds the first dynasty of indigenous kings.

CHAPTER EIGHT

THE TITANS ARRIVE

Ah, my Beloved, fill the Cup that clears
TO-DAY of past Regrets and future Fears --
Tomorrow? -- Why, To-morrow I may be
Myself with Yesterday's Sev'n Thousand Years.

From the *Rubaiyat of Omar Khayyam* trans. by Edward FitzGerald

The civilising of archaic Egypt by time-shifters from 'the future' was elsewhere repeated. It actually happened somewhat earlier in the valleys of the Tigris and Euphrates rivers, in what is now Iraq, than it did in Egypt, although in most other places it occurred later, sometimes many centuries later. In fact, the very idea of carrying out such a bold undertaking seems to have spread along with the knowledge of how to time-slip. And because our modern world has resulted from the activities of these time-shifters, they brought about the most important piece of social engineering in the history of the human race. The wisdom of what they did, however, is entirely another matter.

The Tigris and Euphrates rivers arise in the Taurus mountains of Armenia and flow in a generally south-easterly direction through the Mesopotamian plain to the Persian Gulf. The region has little rainfall and temperatures can reach 120 degrees F. Because the annual volume of flood water is more variable than that of the Nile, agriculture is only possible by making use of an extensive system of canals, dykes, reservoirs, and dams. In those years when a greater than normal amount of snow falls in the mountains of Armenia, the spring thaw can result in a water run-off large enough to flood the whole of the Mesopotamian plain. Such a catastrophic flood may lie behind the Biblical story of Noah and the building of the Ark.

Like ancient Egypt, Mesopotamia in Neolithic times was

inhabited by primitive hunter-gatherers, who lived mainly in the deltas of the two rivers. But although the region is similar in many ways to the Nile valley, it lacks wood and stone for building and deposits of metallic ores, notably those of tin and copper, both of which are needed to make bronze, and iron. Indeed, the delta dwellers, who called their land Sumer, constructed their homes out of mud and reeds, and lived by catching and eating fish, birds and other small game.

So again, how did it come about that these simple, settled and happy people, who followed a traditional, even idyllic way of life, manage in the course of two or three generations to found the world's first urban civilisation? What prompted them to embark upon such a strange course of action, and who or what guided them during it?

Their records written in cuneiform script supply us with the answer, and it is essentially the same as that given by the hieroglyphic writings of the Egyptians: that is, their knowledge of civilised life and the ability to create it through efficient agricultural production and the building of towns, was given to them by the gods. And although the gods of the Sumerians had different names to those of Egypt, they shared much in common with them. They were said to have arrived suddenly and unexpectedly, they possessed a human form, and they were subject to hunger, disease, lust, and death. This indicates that they were really exceptional human beings who visited the region as civilisers and who were later deified.

In Sumerian myth the world as we know it was created by Enlil or 'Lord Air', the child of An, the sky, and Ki, the earth, who separates the copulating couple at his birth. Later, An and Ki have another child, a son named Enki or 'Lord of the Earth', who becomes the god of wisdom and knowledge. However, despite being styled 'Lord of the Earth', Enki is really the 'god' of the fresh or sweet water that arises from the earth, so-named because he, in his wisdom, introduces well-digging and canal building to the Sumerians. Indeed, like Osiris, Enki is the deity who not only brings order and civilisation to Sumer, but to other places in the Middle East as well. He is represented in stone carvings and statues as a tall, well-built, bearded man clad in a long dress-like robe that reaches down to his feet, and who wears a cone-shaped hat.

We may therefore regard Enki as a time-shifter who arrived in Sumer early in the fourth millennium (about 3800 BC), accompanied by several specialist companions, notably Lahar, Ashnan, Dumuzi, and Kabta. He travelled throughout Sumer teaching farming and agricultural methods to the native inhabitants, which included the manufacture and use of essential tools like the plough, the yoke, and the pickaxe. Lahar, who had a specialist knowledge of cattle and husbandry, instructed them in cattle rearing, while Dumuzi, a master shepherd, showed them how to rear sheep. Ashnan's expertise was in cereals and grain production. He instructed the Sumerians in how to sow wheat, rye and other cereals, and how to harvest the grain and store it. Enki is also credited with introducing the cutting of canals and the irrigation thereby of the land bordering the Tigris and Euphrates rivers. With the help of Kabta, who was later deified as the brick-god, Enki demonstrated how to make sun-dried mud bricks with a brick mould, and how to build houses, temples, granaries, stables, cattle-sheds, and indeed towns and cities with them.

Enki brings a wife, named Ninki, with him from 'the future', on whom he fathers a daughter, Ninsar. Yet without sons, Enki cannot found a dynasty by marrying Ninsar to one of them. He therefore takes the remarkable incestuous step of copulating with Ninsar himself, only to father another daughter, who is named Ninkurra. But undeterred by this, when Ninkurra (who is both his daughter and grand-daughter) reaches puberty, he then copulates with her, only to be disappointed again, for the child is another girl, and is named Uttu, who later becomes deified, like her grandmother Ninsar, as a goddess of plants.

Enki's inability to produce a son necessarily limits the civilising of Sumer to his lifetime, yet his task was made easier by the fact, mentioned above, that he was accompanied by a number of specialists from 'the future'. Legend also says that he brought with him the *me* or the tablets of destiny, which gave him the power to confer the blessings of civilisation on mankind and to establish its fate.

The early legends of the Greeks parallel those of the Sumerians and the Egyptians, in that they record the materialisation out of thin air of several mysterious outsiders, who possess more power and considerably more knowledge than the Neolithic hunter-gatherers they visit. These men and women were evidently all time-shifters, of whom the first to arrive, and whom we can regard as the expedition leader, like Ptah/Ra in Egypt, became known as Uranus after the sky from which he seemingly came. His arrival probably took place in about 1600 BC. After having surveyed the Greek mainland and found that its indigenous people had reached a level of development sufficient to benefit from 'future aid', Uranus next arranged for the incoming of several specialists, whom he is quaintly said to have 'fathered' on Mother Earth. These tough 'shock-troops' were, perhaps not surprisingly, big men, and their task was to impart a basic knowledge of building and metal working, which Uranus, like Ptah, rather oddly supposed were the necessary precursors of civilised life.

Three of these specialists were called Cyclopes, a name which, interestingly enough, means 'ring eyed'. They had the job of showing the natives how to mine tin and copper ores and extract the respective metals from them, how to make bronze from the copper and tin, and how to work the bronze into useful objects. They also gave instruction in stone carving and building with stone. Their reputed possession of only one centrally-placed eye, which is recorded in the old stories, is almost certainly a pre-technological way of describing the single protective glass eye-shield they wore when smelting the ores and working the metal, and when stone-carving. The three other time-shifters who came with them, which legend says had one hundred arms and fifty heads -- they were called the Hundred-handed Ones -- were in reality three groups of fifty men, each group serving as a separate support and defence team for one of the Cyclopes.

This advance party of time-shifters, however, was not a success, due to the fact that neither the Cyclopes nor the

Hundred-handed Ones were sufficiently well-trained or experienced to function effectively in what seems to have been a difficult and hostile environment. Indeed, the armed and aggressive Hundred-handed Ones were more of a liability than a benefit. The Greek poet Hesiod calls them 'insolent', which perhaps best describes how they interacted with the indigenes. Not only did Uranus himself have trouble in keeping them in order, but fearing a mutiny, he was forced to take both them and the Cyclopes out of action by confining them to barracks.

Uranus then brought in the main task force of time-shifters, all big, physically robust and highly trained and motivated individuals, whose collective name, the Titans, is still used today to describe large, powerful people. Exactly how many of them were in this group is uncertain. Hesiod says that there were only twelve, consisting of six men and six women, but as he claims that two of the Titans, namely Cottus and Briareus, had one hundred arms and fifty heads, they were probably two support teams of fifty individuals each, like the Hundred-handed Ones. If so, the Titans formed an education group of ten teachers, four men and six women, trained in basic agricultural methods, backed up by one hundred support staff.

Legend also says the Titans were brothers and sisters (the six females are correctly called Titanesses or Titanides), the children of Uranus and Mother Earth, but this notion surely derives from their sudden emergence from a large cave or a similar naturally enclosed place, like a valley, wherein they had materialised. Their leader was code-named Cronus, meaning 'the Crow'.

But trouble happened even before the Titans began their mission. It came from the disgruntled Cyclopes and their three support teams, who were angry at their dismissal from the project. They made secret contact with Cronus, poured out their resentment against Uranus, who seemingly lacked both tact and leadership skills, and suggested that if an 'accident' happened to Uranus, Cronus could assume command, which would be advantageous to them all. The fact that Cronus agreed to do as they suggested indicates that he had already lost confidence in Uranus, possibly because Uranus had somewhat bizarrely sent in the three Cyclopes, who were metal-work and building instructors and who each required fifty helpers, ahead of the agricultural team of Titans, which to Cronus was like putting the cart before the horse. He doubtlessly suspected that the mission would fail if Uranus remained in charge.

Because the 'accident' had to be serious and dramatic without being fatal -- a minor injury could have been dealt with by the support team medics, while Uranus's death would have led to a full enquiry -- Cronus came up with the ingenious plan of wounding the commander in the genitals with his sickle, which could, he believed, be easily accomplished when he was demonstrating the use of that agricultural tool to the natives. And this is what almost certainly happened, despite Hesiod claiming that Cronus castrated his 'father' when he was asleep. Rather, one day in a field Cronus simply swung his sickle a little too enthusiastically and slashed Uranus where it hurts most, possibly severing or partially severing his scrotum, which caused the loss of a lot of blood and much pain to the unfortunate victim. And naturally, the injured man immediately agreed to time-slip himself back to the future for treatment, leaving the apologetic Cronus in command. The scheme thus far had worked brilliantly.

But once Cronus had taken that step he knew he could not leave himself vulnerable to betrayal by the Cyclopes and their support teams. He probably also suspected that they would either alienate the locals and jeopardise the whole project by insisting on prematurely pushing ahead with the building and ore-extraction/metal-work programme or they would threaten the future by running wild and by fraternising too closely with the local women, or even by doing both. And as they could not be allowed to return home, they therefore had to be taken out of action. Cronus and his fellow Titans accomplished this by blocking the entrance of the large cave in which they slept, thus imprisoning them.

That done, Cronus began work on the great agricultural project, which he clearly saw was the only practical first step towards civilised life. The ten specialists paired off, each Titan teaming with a Titaness, although one pair of necessity consisted of two Titanesses, and they went to different parts of Thessaly, the region of Greece where the project was centred, each taking twenty support workers with them. The partner Cronus chose he nicknamed Rhea, meaning 'earth', for he also intended sowing his seed in her along the way. Cronus and Rhea remained at the base camp HQ, which was probably situated in the southern Othrys mountains, from where he directed operations, received regular reports of progress made, distributed quantities of seed, and taught the Neolithic hunter-gatherers of the locality the elements of agriculture. Rhea, like the other Titanesses, worked with the local women, showing them how to sow wheat, barley and other grains, and various vegetables, in the ground that the men had cleared of scrub and had ploughed. Animal husbandry and the use of manure as a fertiliser was also taught, as was the building of pens, fences, barns, and store rooms.

The enterprise was of course a long term project, and each Titan duo remained with the tribe they contacted for a whole year, showing them how to deal with, where possible, every problem that arose and familiarizing them with each of the many steps between sowing and harvesting, or the birth of an animal and its killing for the table. The harvest was the most important part of the process, because it was only then that the results and benefits of all the previous hard work became plain. Indeed, the work of the first year would have been made doubly hard by the fact that the locals had to continue to hunt game or forage for fruit and berries while their crops and livestock were growing. Then once the harvest was in and crop storage introduced, the Titan pairs moved to a new location and tribal group, although they maintained contact with the first, visiting them regularly to check how things were progressing and to offer support and encouragement. They may even have left two of their support team with the tribe to act as advisers and go-betweens.

We can get some idea of the length of time that Cronus and the other Titans/Titanesses stayed working on this project from the fact that Cronus fathered six children on Rhea, three boys and three girls, and that he continued as group leader until the boys had reached adulthood, which indicates a period of at least a quarter of a century, possibly longer. The teams were hard working and dedicated, and they not only brought great benefits to the aboriginal Greeks but they came among them as helpers, not conquerors. Hence it is hardly surprising that the so-called reign of Cronus was looked back upon in later years as a Golden Age, when people were happy, well-fed, longer-lived, and more secure. It seems that much of Cronus's success was due to the fact that he did not force the natives to abandon their traditional way of life, but simply showed them how more food could be grown or reared, trusting that the merits of his methods would speak for themselves, which is what they did.

Cronus was delighted when his agricultural scheme was jogging along nicely, yet as the years passed he became more and more worried that his children, whom tradition names as Hestia, Demeter, Hera, Poseidon, Hades, and Zeus, would not only take over from him but would introduce practises that he did not understand and which he regarded as being of negative civilising value. The six children had all been sent back to 'the future' at intervals to receive their education, and had been trained there to begin the second phase of the civilisation project, which included ship building and the use of the sea for trade and commerce; the mining of metal ores and precious stones; and the introduction of formalised religion. It was left to the three young men to decide which of these activities they wanted to take charge of, unlike the girls, who had been trained for specialist tasks. Hestia had studied domestic architecture, fire-lighting, and cooking, and Hera had been given the job of introducing monogamous marriages, midwifery, and the proper care and training of children. Only Demeter was assigned an agricultural role, but her wish to concentrate on grain growing was at odds with Cronus's desire to continue with his mixed farming/hunter-gatherer policy.

Indeed, Cronus seems to have believed that the sea-faring activities would eventually result in the building of navies for use in warfare and colonisation; that the extraction of ores and precious stones would promote dishonesty, cupidity, the manufacture of arms, and as a natural development, armed conflict; while the last, the introduction of formalised religion, would result in more superstition, prompt the construction of expensive temples rather than farm buildings and homes, and provide a spurious reason for going to war. With these dangers so evident and so potentially dangerous, Cronus took the extraordinary step of restraining his children by locking them up in an underground dungeon, and when he was asked where they were, he jocularly replied that he had eaten them; it was a joke that came back to haunt him, for his children later made use of it to represent him as a cannibal and thus to excuse his overthrow by them.

They remained imprisoned until their mother Rhea, who thought their treatment unfair, contrived to release Zeus, the youngest and most spirited of her three sons. The young man immediately left Greece for the safety of Crete, the isle of his birth (Cronus and the pregnant Rhea were on a visit there at the time, assessing the civilisation project that had been underway there for many years), and where he hid and planned the usurpation of his father. His opportunity came sooner than he expected, for Cronus, hearing that his son had gone to Crete, went to the island to look for him. He made the mistake, however, of taking his wife with him and his five other captive children, whom he kept from running away by chaining them to large stones. For Rhea betrayed him again. She smuggled Zeus into the camp, where he secretly added a somniferous drug to a mug of his father's favourite honeyed drink. Cronus unsuspectingly drank the potion, and it wasn't long before he was dead to the world. That gave Zeus the opportunity to release his siblings, and together they made their escape back to Thessaly.

Because Cronus's sons and daughters were arrogantly convinced that the civilisation project had to proceed in the directions that they had been trained to take it, the only way they could do this was to make war on, and to thereby overthrow, the agriculturalist Titans, their children and their many loyal supporters. It was a long, bitter conflict resembling that between Horus and Set, which went on for ten years. Most of the action took place in Thessaly, Zeus and his siblings setting up their base camp on Mount Olympus on the region's northern border, while the Titans established themselves in the Othrys mountains to the south. But Zeus's group fared badly until they treacherously released the imprisoned Cyclopes and the so-called Hundred-handed Ones, who jumped at the chance of taking their revenge on Cronus. The Cyclopes helped Zeus by making him a type of artillery weapon called a 'thunderbolt' which caused havoc among the Titans and the gentle farmers. The forces ranged against Cronus were now too powerful, and he fled for safety to Italy, where to his everlasting credit he continued with his agricultural mission among the indigenous people, who took their name -- Latins -- from the fact that he hid himself among them (*lateo* means 'to hide'), and who in turn lovingly nicknamed him 'the sower' or Saturn.

Having won the war, the victorious sons of Cronus threw lots to decide which of the above-mentioned spheres of activity they should each be responsible for, and Poseidon drew the ship building and maritime concession, Hades the metal ores and precious stones extraction concession, while Zeus, who had played such a pivotal role in the war with the Titans, both gained the religious concession and took overall charge of the whole mission. Their sisters Hestia, Demeter and Hera went ahead with introducing the particular skills for which they had been trained.   This was the beginning of the myth of the twelve Olympian 'gods' with which most people are familiar. For Zeus, like Shu, Geb and the other time-slippers in Egypt, married his sister Hera, on whom he fathered Hebe, Hephaestus, and the twins Eris and Ares. He also had an affair with Demeter, who gave birth to a son, Iacchus, and a daughter named Core, although the latter is better known as Persephone, who married his brother Hades. Another affair with a Titaness named Metis resulted in the birth of Athene; while he fathered Apollo and Artemis on the Titaness Leto, and Hermes on Maia.

In these unions Zeus was careful to mate with other

time-shifters, so that he did not introduce new individuals into the native population, whom he knew had the potential to alter 'the future'. Yet Zeus, having like Thoth a demanding libido, behaved irresponsibly later on and slept with several women of the time, such as Danae, who bore him the famous hero Perseus. In this way Zeus helped undermine the raison d'etre of the civilisation project in Greece.

It is unnecessary to describe all the dubious benefits that Zeus and his siblings, and later his children, who were all time-slipped 'back to the future' for their education -- which explains why Hermes, for example, and Apollo, who was, like Horus, prematurely born, are said to have grown with astonishing speed -- brought to the world, as these are recorded in the stories about their lives. But I will mention Hermes, who, like Thoth, introduced the alphabet and writing, along with the musical scale, boxing and gymnastics, astronomy, weights and measures, the use of knuckle-bones for gaming and divination, and the cultivation of the olive, to name but a few of his gifts. Yet their various activities on earth, which include wars fought, injuries received, love involvements with the natives, treacheries, contests of one sort and another, and, where Apollo and Poseidon are concerned, working as labourers for an Asiatic king as punishment for a misdeed, show that they were real human beings, not gods, who came from 'the future' and who, like the other time-slippers, helped obliterate their own society through both their work as civilisers and their irresponsible sexual behaviour. This explains why no time shifters after Uranus and his helpmates the Cyclopes, the Hundred-handed Ones, and the Titans, arrived from the future, and hence why 'the gods' seemingly died.

It was mentioned earlier that Cronus, after his defeat by Zeus and his other children, fled to central Italy. There he took refuge with a powerful king named Janus. The monarch was so impressed with Cronus's bearing and knowledge that he offered to share his throne with him. This gave Cronus an unrivalled opportunity to carry on his mission by civilising his benefactor's barbaric subjects, which he began by instructing them in agriculture, vine cultivation, animal husbandry, and forestry.

This work, as previously indicated, earned him the nickname of Saturn, and led to Janus's realm being called Latium. Indeed, so successful was he, and so mild, beneficial and popular was his rule, that the time he spent in Latium was regarded, as it had been in Greece, as a Golden Age, when everyone lived free from want and care. The joys of Saturn's Golden Age were celebrated among the Romans each year at a festival called the Saturnalia, which began on 17 December and lasted for one week. Saturn is characteristically represented in art as a bearded man clad in a long robe, holding a scythe in his right hand.

Equally interestingly, a group of immigrants called Etruscans settled in Latium during the eighth century BC, following their forced departure from Lydia in Asia Minor. They were familiar with agriculture, metal-working and so on, and hence were a civilised people. Yet their legends claim that they were visited by a strange dwarf-like being that one day sprang from a furrow in a field being ploughed by a farmer named Tarchon.

The unexpected visitor had the size and the face of a child, yet the long grey beard and hair and the manner of an old man. Tarchon's cries of alarm quickly brought his fellow Etruscans to the scene, and at their arrival the dwarf told them his name was Tages and that he had been sent there to teach them how to live properly. He then imparted to his listeners, who hurriedly recorded what he said on wax tablets, a body of knowledge known as the Tagetic doctrine, which outlined the laws of property, the nature of the gods and the structure of the universe, and a method of divination by interpreting the livers of sacrificed animals, called *haruspicy*. That done, he stepped back into the furrow and vanished.

This sounds a wholly fanciful tale, although when we remember that several recent time shifters, such as Charlotte Moberly and Eleanor Jourdain, have only remained in 'the past' for brief periods, it is not as unlikely as it at first seems. And the Etruscans had no doubt that it happened. They regarded Tages' coming and the Tagetic doctrine he imparted as the central event of their new life in Italy, from which the whole of their remarkable culture evolved. Furthermore, Tages' dwarfish form gives him a surprising connection with Ptah, the first time shifter to visit Egypt, who while generally represented as a normal-sized man, is sometimes also portrayed as an ugly, deformed dwarf, much like Tages.

What is likewise interesting about the time-shifters and their children is that most of the men are described as being tall, bearded, fair-skinned and middle-aged, and who wear a long robe and often a curious hat. Hermes, for example, was thus originally portrayed, although in classical times it became fashionable to give him a more youthful appearance. And his hat was originally round, with a wide brim, somewhat like a bowler, yet it was later turned into a winged helmet called a petasus.

The time-shifters also typically carried a staff, which was not simply a wooden pole on which they could lean when walking or which served as a symbol of their authority, but which instead possessed certain powers which could be utilised when needed. This suggests that it was some type of advanced technological device. We do not know anything about its interior design, except that gold was one of the elements used to make it. However, one time-slipped staff did survive until at least the second century AD, when it was inspected by the writer Pausanias at the shrine of Chaeronea in Greece, where it was kept.

This particular staff was said to have been made by Hephaestus, the son of Zeus and Hera, who had been trained in metal work and in specialty manufacture in 'the future', and who then gave it to his father. Zeus thereupon made a gift of it to his son Hermes, the half-brother of Hephaestus, by whom it was used to induce sleep and also, more remarkably, to revivify the dead.

Eventually Hermes, it is said, gave the staff to a king's son named Pelops, whose father was the famous Tantalus, who was the son of Zeus and of Pluto, the daughter of Zeus's own grandparents, Cronus and Rhea. Hence Tantalus was of wholly incestuous time-slipper stock. He was the king of either Argos or Corinth, and was close to his father Zeus, who allowed him to attend the banquets of 'the gods' on Mount Olympus and elsewhere, at which the time-slippers' special food and drink known as nectar and ambrosia, which was brought from 'the future', was consumed. But Tantalus appears to have failed to respect the secrets he had learned from Zeus on these occasions, for he not only passed some of them on to his friends among the Greeks but he also shared the food he stole from the time-slipped incomers with them.

What happened next is reminiscent of Seth's dismemberment of Osiris, for when Tantalus promised to give a banquet for the time-slipped 'gods' he took the extraordinarily gruesome step of killing and cutting up Pelops and adding the pieces of his son to the stew he made. The reason for this terrible act was probably to make those time-slipped eat human flesh, as it was part of their mission to turn the barbaric natives away from their traditional practice of cannibalism. Fortunately, however, those attending the dinner realised what had been set before them and declined to eat it, with the exception of Demeter, who ate Pelops' left shoulder. These two actions, that of betraying the time-shifters' secrets and of trying to make them unwittingly into cannibals, led Zeus to kill Tantalus, and then, so it is said, to condemn his soul to the torment of eternal hunger and thirst. Afterwards Zeus, like Isis before him had also done, collected up the uneaten portions of Pelops' corpse, which Hermes and Rhea united and brought back to life, Demeter contributing an artificial shoulder made of ivory for the one that she had unfortunately eaten.

The revivified Pelops in due course passed the staff on to Atreus, king of Argos, from whom it came into the hands of his brother Thyestes, when he seized the throne from him, and then became the property of Atreus's son Agamemnon when he and his brother Menelaus ousted Thyestes. This staff was at the time widely regarded as the only genuine artefact made by Hephaestus, the great-grandson of Uranus, still in existence, and Pausanias says of it:

> They have a cult of this staff, which they call the Shaft.
> There must be some divinity about it to explain the

glory it brings to human beings . . . It has no public temple, but the priest in each year keeps the staff in his house. Sacrifices are offered to it every day, and it has a table full of every kind of meat and sweet-cake.

Now Agamemnon became the commander-in-chief of the Greek forces during the Trojan War, which took place between 1198-1188 BC. The staff was therefore given to him sometime prior to its start, perhaps in 1203 BC or thereabouts. If Pelops, Atreus and Thyestes possessed it between them for fifty years, then Pelops would have acquired the staff from Hermes in about 1253 BC. We cannot know how long Hermes owned it beforehand, but as he is always portrayed as carrying a staff, it would seem that he was seen with it over a sufficiently long period to become closely associated with it. But if we take 1600 BC as the approximate starting date for the civilisation mission in Greece, then Hermes will probably have been given the staff by Zeus at the close of the sixteenth century BC, say one hundred years before he passed it on to Pelops, that is, in 1400 BC.

I shall be discussing these mysterious staffs at greater length in the next chapter, as the powers that some, or all, of them apparently possessed were more destructive than those mentioned above. And as we shall see, the date when Hermes gave his staff to Pelops is close to that when the so-called 'rod of God' was acquired by Moses.

Another contributor to the time-slipper civilisation project was Triptolemus (or 'thrice daring'), the son of either king Celeus of Eleusis in Attica by his wife Metaneira, or of Poseidon and Mother Earth, and who was taught the art of agriculture by Demeter. She then provided him with seed corn and a plough and sent him out into to the world to teach cultivation and grain growing to all whom he met. When Triptolemus returned to Eleusis he became its king and founded there the famous mysteries in honour of Demeter.

Perhaps more famous is Aristaeus, whose name means 'the best', the son of Apollo and a Greek woman named Cyrene, who later became the queen of the famous Libyan city named after her, where Aristaeus was born. Legend recounts how as a baby he was given into the care of the Hours and Mother Earth, and later into that of the Myrtle nymphs, who taught him various agricultural skills, notably the cultivation of the olive, bee-keeping, cheese-making, and shepherding. This early association with not only the Hours, but also with Mother Earth and the Myrtle nymphs, whose tree, the myrtle, is a symbol of death, suggest that Aristaeus was transported into 'the future' for his education, thereby vanishing from his own time for a number of years. This explains why nothing is known of his childhood and early youth.

On his return, Aristaeus began his agricultural mission in Greece, where he travelled widely teaching the natives what he had learned, especially the practice of apiculture or bee-keeping for which he became celebrated. He then went further afield to Sicily, Sardinia, and possibly Crete, and later to Thrace and Bulgaria. Yet he blotted his copybook by attempting to rape Eurydice, the lover of Orpheus, who stepped on a snake as she fled from him and died from its poisonous bite. For this accidental killing 'the gods' punished him by destroying his bees, and he remained without bees until, on the advice of an oracle, he performed a sacrifice to the Dryad nymphs, Eurydice's companions, upon which the insects were miraculously restored to him. Sometime afterwards, Aristaeus went to live on the slopes of Mount Haemus, situated in the Rhodope mountain range of southern Bulgaria and Thrace, where he founded a city named Aristeum. But one day he mysteriously and unaccountably vanished on the mountain, from which time on he was worshipped as a god, it being assumed that he had been taken up to heaven, although he was almost certainly taken off to 'the future'.

Dionysus, later to become the Greek god of wine, was sent back from 'the future' specifically to teach viniculture, the making of wine, and the enjoyment of wine drinking. He was not, however, a member of the Greek time-slipper mission, as he apparently manifested from 'the future' on mount Nysa in Ethiopia, despite later being called the son of

Zeus and Semele. Yet as the name Semele derives from a Phrygian earth-goddess called Zemele, while Zeus was, like Uranus before him, the 'god' of the sky, this indicates that he, like his fellow time-slippers, materialized out of thin air, probably in a cave on the above-mentioned mountain. His name, Dionysus, means 'god of Nysa'. He was the most active and enthusiastic of the time-shifters, travelling as he did throughout the ancient world, from north-east Africa, to Greece, the Middle East, and as far east as India. And while he is represented in later times as a clean-shaven and somewhat effeminate youth, he was originally and more accurately portrayed as a middle-aged, bearded man clad in long flowing robes and carrying a staff called a thyrsus. He was accompanied on his journeys by his tutor Silenus and a number of assistants, and often by crowds of drunken men and women. When island-hopping in the Aegean Dionysus met and fell in love with a beautiful young woman named Ariadne, whom he married and on whom, contrary to regulations, he fathered several children. However, his marriage enables us to date his mission to the thirteenth century BC. Sometime later, perhaps not surprisingly, he was recalled to 'the future', and he vanished near Thebes. His strange and sudden departure, coupled with the pleasant social benefits of wine making and drinking that he spread so widely, soon led to him being regarded as a deity rather than the time-slipped human being he undoubtedly was.

Several more recent time-slip missions were likewise carried out in Central and South America, as many of the stories told by the diverse peoples of that vast continent relate how they were visited by outsiders, who lived among them for lengthy periods and whom they regarded as gods. These uninvited but most welcome newcomers taught them certain technical and scientific skills, various arts and crafts, and gave them their laws, thereby enabling them to live together in a civilised manner. And as we shall see, the descriptions given of them closely match those of the time-slipped visitors I have already mentioned.

The Aztecs of Mexico claimed that when they were uncivilised barbarians a god named Quetzalcoatl came among then and lived with them for several years, during which time he taught them the elements of agriculture, notably the cultivation of Indian corn and cotton, the extraction and use of metals, the building of houses, the study of astronomy and the making of accurate calendars, and the art of government. Quetzalcoatl's evident manifestation out of thin air at the start of his mission led in due course to him being worshipped as the 'god of the air' by the Aztecs. His mission, as far as we can date it, probably took place in the first century AD and lasted for several years. In appearance, Quetzalcoatl was said to be a tall, white-skinned man, who had long dark hair and a long beard. And so successful was he, that his time spent among the Aztecs, like that of Cronus/Saturn among the Greeks and Latins, was looked back to as a Golden Age, when food was abundant and life was much easier and happier than it had been before or, indeed, it was afterwards. But nevertheless, it appears that Quetzalcoatl stepped outside his brief in some unexplained way, and was forced to prematurely end his mission. What happened then is unusual, because instead of returning immediately to 'the future', he left Mexico by boat, promising to return one day, and sailed east into the Gulf of Mexico.

We may perhaps surmise that the man who was Quetzalcoatl perished somewhere out to sea, for he never went back to Mexico, despite his return being yearned for by the later Aztecs, and as it still is by native Mexicans. But unfortunately, his promise to return was more of a curse than a comfort, because when Hernando Cortez and his fellow bearded, white-skinned Spaniards arrived on that fateful and misnamed Good Friday, the 21 April 1519, it was generally believed that the good and benevolent Quetzalcoatl had at long last come back. The Aztecs welcomed the Spaniards with flowers, fruits, and great rejoicing, and too late discovered that they were really a gang of thugs who were only interested in their gold. Their intense disappointment, following as it did so quickly upon their cruelly raised hopes, took the heart (no pun intended) out of them, and their empire was soon defeated by the musketry and the cannon firing of the Spaniards, and by their armoured and horse-riding cavaliers, despite their small numbers. This debacle was clearly another time-slip own-goal.

Similarly, the legends of the Mayas of nearby Yucutan recount how they were visited by a 'god' named Kukulcan, whose name in their tongue means 'bird snake', and it is fascinating to note that the name is virtually identical in meaning to Quetzalcoatl or 'feathered serpent' of the Aztecs. Kukulcan visited Yucutan comparatively recently, probably in AD 967, and he arrived somewhat unusually by boat along with nineteen assistants. In common with other time-slipped persons they were all white-skinned, bearded and wore long robes. Hence they could not have been, as most archaeologists claim, visiting Aztecs, because the Aztecs were, like other Central and South American peoples, a brown-skinned and largely beardless race. Kukulcan's companions likewise all possessed special skills which led to them being individually regarded at a later date as 'gods' of agriculture, fishing, metal work, arts and crafts, and so on. Kukulcan, as the expedition's leader, was responsible for imparting to the Mayas a number of sensible and practical laws, which formed the framework of the civilised society he helped them create. Then, after remaining in Yucutan for twenty years, Kukulcan and his party of time-shifters re-embarked aboard their boat and sailed east towards the rising sun.

Yet the Mayas, so their legends reveal, had previously been visited by another 'god' called Itzamna, whom they said was the son of Humab Ku, the sun, and his wife Ixazalouh, the water. This pairing of sun and water, which closely accords with that of sky and earth, suggests that Itzamna was a time-shifter of the traditional type, who doubtlessly came directly from 'the future' and so manifested, or so it would have appeared, out of thin air, perhaps in or beside a sunlit lake. His arrival was much earlier than that of Kukulcan, and probably occurred in the first or second century AD, at about the same date, in other words, as Quetzalcoatl's among the Aztecs. Itzamna taught agriculture and irrigation to the Mayas, as well as building and architecture, mathematics and astronomy, and perhaps most important of all, hieroglyphic writing, which enabled them to record their observations of the heavens, their laws, their religious beliefs, and their history. Because Ixazalouh, Itzamna's mother, was said to have been the inventor of weaving, this may mean that Itzamna was accompanied by various time-slipped companions, some of whom were probably women, who taught such skills. Another talent supposedly possessed by Itzamna was his ability to reanimate the dead, which as we have noted is reported of several other time-shifters.

The Incas of Peru also claimed that when they were barbarians they were visited by a god, who not only came and lived among them and taught them the prerequisites of civilisation, but who was, like Itzamna, the son of the sun. The name of this man was Viracocha, and he apparently emerged, again like Itzamna, from a lake, namely Titicaca, which is Peru's largest. This again suggests that he manifested from 'the future' either in or beside the lake. His close association with lake Titicaca led to him being regarded in later times as the god of water generally and of rain, and of the fertilising powers of that element, which is why he was said to have no physical body, yet he could, like water cascading down a mountain slope, run very fast. However, he is portrayed as being a middle-aged, bearded, fair-skinned man, dressed in a long white robe and carrying a staff, in common with most of the other time-slipped visitors I have mentioned. And neither did he come alone, but was accompanied by his sister, Mama-Cocha, whom he married, and by a number of white-skinned, auburn-haired companions, known as the Viracochas.

Viracocha carried out exactly the same mission among the uncivilised Incas as his fellow time-slip travellers did elsewhere. He taught the natives farming and animal husbandry, the extraction of metal from its ores and metallurgy, building and architecture, the principles of engineering, and the art of hieroglyphic writing, while the Viracochas actually built, although presumably assisted by the Incas, a number of walled cities, roads, and bridges, as well as marking out, or so it is said, the remarkable and gigantic line figures at Nazca. Viracocha's activities required him to travel throughout the Inca territory, and because he always treated the natives kindly and considerately, and with infinite patience, he came to be greatly loved by them. He was also apparently able to heal the sick by touching them. Then, after living among the Incas for several years, he concluded his mission by appointing a king over them, named Allcavica, from whom the later Incas claimed their descent. That done, and upon having promised to return at a future date, Viracocha and his followers left by disappearing into the water of lake Titicaca. But like Quetzalcoatl, he has so far not reappeared.

The Incas eventually founded a vast empire that extended from Ecuador in the north, through Peru and Bolivia, to as far south as northern Chile and Argentina. But while their empire was vast in size and highly organised, it was despotically ruled by one man, the Inca or king, who was regarded as a living god, in whom all power lay and who made all the decisions. This over-reliance on a single individual had disastrous consequences, for following the death of king Huayna Capac in 1525, a civil war was fought between his two sons, Huascar and Atahuallpa, and their respective followers. Atahuallpa won, yet before he could properly establish himself, he was attacked and captured by Francisco Pizarro and his men. A huge ransom was demanded for Atahuallpa's release, but when it had been paid Pizarro treacherously put him to death, on 29 August 1533. Pizarro next marched on Cuzco, the Inca capital, which he besieged and captured, and thus speedily brought about the downfall of the rudderless Inca empire, whose overthrow had been predicted by Viracocha as happening during the reign of the thirteenth Inca, which Atahuallpa was. However, readers will be gratified to know that the despicable Pizarro was assassinated by fellow Spanish thugs at Lima in June 1541.

Lastly, I shall mention the Chibcha natives of the Cundinamarca plateau of central Columbia, who said that in ancient times when they lived as savages they were visited by a wise old man called Bochica, whom they believed was a god and who was not only of a different race but who sported a long and thick beard, like the previously mentioned time slippers. He came among them with his wife, a beautiful white woman named Chia, and a number of followers.

Bochica taught the Chibchas how to plant crops and harvest them, how to build simple huts for shelter, how to live together peaceably in accordance with civilised laws, and how to worship 'the gods'. Yet Chia, his wife, did not agree with what he was doing and continually tried to frustrate his civilising activities. This suggests of course that she understood the dangers inherent in the operation. But when she failed to stop him, she angrily caused the river Funzi to flood the whole plain through which it flowed, destroying not only the crops growing there, but many of the Chibchas as well. This act of sabotage so angered Bochica that he exiled her, so the legend says, from the earth to the sky, or in other words, he had her transported back to 'the future'. Bochica, however, remained among the Chibchas for many years, then when his mission was completed, he returned with his companions to the time from which they had come.

CHAPTER NINE

THE BIBLICAL TIME-SHIFTER

Where lies the land to which the ship would go?
Far, far ahead, is all her seamen know.
And where the land she travels from? Away,
Far, far behind, is all that they can say.

From an untitled poem by Arthur Hugh Clough

In the previous two chapters I have recounted how the then primitive peoples of such different and far-flung regions as Egypt, the Middle East, Greece, Italy, Central and South America, and elsewhere, were visited, so their legends record, by mysterious outsiders who lived among them and taught them the skills necessary to raise themselves from a state of barbarism to one that was generally more advanced and civilised. These bringers of civilisation usually came as a small, sometimes mixed-sex group, led by a middle-aged man, who is typically described as being bearded, long-haired and fair-complexioned, clad in a long robe and the bearer of a staff. The group stay and work with the natives for a number of years, sometimes even for several generations. At first its members carefully avoid any sexual involvement with the indigenes and mate only with one another, including their own sisters, which suggests they are forbidden from fraternising with them, although their descendants, who are born in the places concerned, become more cavalier about this and start to pair with local people and have children by them. Yet such interbreeding turns out to be a fatal mistake, because after it happens the visitors -- who are regarded as gods by those they help -- vanish and never return.

I have further argued that these strange civilisers did not come from outer space or from Atlantis, or even from some other unknown centre of civilisation, but were instead people who arrived from what we call 'the future'. This means that they had discovered how to step completely out of their own time, to undergo, in other words, Past and Future Encounters of the Fourth Kind, which ability they used to explore the very distant past as well as more recent times, and to return to their present and to possibly venture even further into 'the future' beyond that. Their civilising missions were apparently prompted by a desire to increase the rate of human social and technical evolution, not for altruistic reasons but solely to benefit their own 'future' society. That is, they used their time-slipping ability not to bring about a positive change in a past Dark Age period, as did the hero of Mark Twain's *A Yankee at the Court of King Arthur*, but for an altogether more ambitious end.

Yet civilisation is not only about people being able to farm and grow sufficient food, mine and use metals, build houses, use writing, and to express themselves artistically through poetry, sculpture, music, painting and design, and so on. At the outset, it requires barbarians to lose their tribal hunter-gatherer identity and allegiances and their ancient suspicions and hatreds, and to then live harmoniously and cooperatively together in larger numbers. They are helped in this development by the adoption of a common deity or deities, which is a role the time-slippers accepted for themselves and perhaps encouraged, but equally importantly civilisation can only grow within a codified system of laws that tell people how they can and cannot behave, and what is required of them, and one which is ideally given to them by their gods so that it has an accepted religious and moral legitimacy.

I have mentioned that several of the time-shifter 'gods' gave laws to the barbaric people with whom they resided and worked, although they perhaps understandably concentrated more on teaching their pupils how to do things, like grow crops and build houses, than they did on their moral education, especially once they had successfully turned them from cannibalism. However, there was one time-slip visitor who put law and morality at the top of his list, perhaps because he feared that without strict, apparently God-given laws, the people with whom he interacted, the Hebrews or

Israelites, would otherwise lose their identity in the populous and turbulent region where they lived, the Middle East.

The time-slipper in question was called Jehovah (originally Yahweh, meaning 'he that is'), and the Hebrews Jehovah initially worked with were nomadic animal-herders, living on the outskirts of societies that had already become civilised, like those of Egypt and Mesopotamia. This meant he did not have to concern himself with teaching them about the physical aspects of civilisation, for they could learn about those, with his assistance, from the civilised societies already in existence, but he could instead concentrate on providing them with a system of laws and a moral code that would help preserve them as a group and which they could pass on to others. And we are fortunate in having, in the Old Testament, a detailed account of Jehovah's activities in this regard, which tells us that he did not live intimately among the Hebrews as a known leader, like the other time-slip arrivals did with those they adopted, but instead established a more distant, intermittent and more God-like relationship with them.

The notion of Jehovah being a time-slipped individual might seem outrageous or even blasphemous to some readers, but when we look at what the Old Testament says about him, we cannot but be struck by the similarities that exist between him and his time-slipped compatriots. After all, why do many people today still think of God as a middle-aged, bearded man dressed in a long robe? This is not a laughable image plucked out of the air, for as we have seen it is the description given, by several different and unconnected racial groups, to the leader of the time-slipping 'gods' who visited them.

The Old Testament relates that Jehovah often communicated with different Hebrew patriarchs through dreams and visions, or sometimes as a disembodied voice, which atheists can easily dismiss as hallucinations, yet on those few occasions when he is seen he is described as having the form of a man. And in common with the other time-slippers he sometimes comes with helpmates, the first of which, who are called 'the sons of God', were probably his actual male children, while those who follow them are referred to as 'angels'. The word angel (from the Greek *angelos*), means 'messenger', nothing more and when it is used in the Bible it does not refer to a divine being having one or more pairs of wings, which is an image angels only acquired in the early Middle Ages. In fact the angels mentioned in the Old Testament are described as looking just like other men, which is why they are often not recognised as being in any way out of the ordinary at first, and they bring messages or commands from Jehovah, hence their descriptive title. And such time-slipping assistants had normal sexual urges, which prompt 'the sons of God', in common with their colleagues elsewhere, to mate with the women they encounter.

> And it came to pass, when men began to multiply on the face of the earth, and daughters were born unto them, That the sons of God saw the daughters of men that they were fair; and they took them wives of all which they choose.' (*Genesis* 6, vs.1-2).

This lustful behaviour, which as we have noted is dangerously against the rules, apparently prompts their father Jehovah to send them back to 'the future', as the 'sons of God' play no further part in the civilising mission. Rather, the later assistants of Jehovah are invariably referred to as 'angels' and they present themselves either singly or in pairs. This means that Jehovah was forced to cut his coat according to his cloth, for having had to get rid of the core family members of his team who would not leave the local women alone, he was left with only a few 'angelic' helpers, perhaps half a dozen at the most. This may well have prevented him from organising the physical civilising of the Hebrews, which would have required far more manpower, and obliged him instead to concentrate on their moral education.

This Jehovah did with a vengeance. Angered by the disruption of his mission and seemingly blaming Hebrew women as much as his own sons for the latter's indiscretions, he malevolently loads the Hebrew nation down with a mass of legislation governing every single aspect of their lives, which in its extent and tedious nit-picking detail has only recently been rivalled by that emanating from the European Union. Yet ironically he is the least civilised of the civilisers, for he constantly behaves like an irritable, short-tempered, single-minded tyrant, killing those who displease him, insanely jealous of other time-slipping 'gods', and overly keen to present himself as the only time-shifter who really matters. Indeed, such is his elevated view of himself that he seemingly comes to believe he is the one True God. Furthermore, it is possible, considering these extreme mental traits accentuated by the loss of his sons and the emotional support they could have given him that he is suffering from a depressive condition verging on psychosis

Let us now look at the first recorded encounter between Jehovah and the man he has selected to work with, namely Abram, which took place in about 1895 BC: Jehovah himself, depending upon the unknown number and ages of his sons, may well at that time have been in his fifties.

> And when Abram was ninety years old and nine, the Lord appeared unto Abram, and said unto him, I am Almighty God; walk before me, and be thou perfect . . . And Abram fell on his face: and God talked with him . . . (*Genesis* 17, 1-3).

Jehovah tells Abram that he will make a covenant with him, that his name shall no longer be Abram but Abraham, that he will give him and his descendants the land of Canaan, and that he and they, to mark the covenant between them, must all be circumcised.

And next, after having promised that Abraham's elderly wife Sarai, thence to be called Sarah, shall bear a son, 'he left off talking with him, and God went up from Abraham.'

The sudden arrival of Jehovah and his departure by apparently rising and disappearing into the air is exactly the same as those of the time-shifter 'gods' described in the last two chapters.

The next interaction is longer and takes place when

Abraham is back with his family living in a tent at Mamre, and which happens later in the same year, although this time Jehovah is accompanied by two male companions:

> And the Lord appeared unto him in the plains of Mamre: and he (Abraham) sat in the tent door in the heat of the day; And he lift up his eyes and looked, and, lo, three men stood by him: and when he saw them, he ran to meet them from the tent door, and bowed himself toward the ground, And said, My Lord, if now I have found favour in thy sight, pass not away, I pray thee, from thy servant. Let a little water be fetched, and wash your feet, and rest yourselves under a tree. (*Genesis* 18, vs. 1-4)

This passage unequivocally describes Jehovah as having a human form, of being, in other words, a man, and he comes not alone but with two other men, who are fellow time-slipped companions. Abraham immediately tells his wife Sarah to prepare them a meal, and his visitors' humanity is further shown by their willingness to wait for a calf to be selected and killed, then for it to be cooked, and lastly to eat it when it's ready, sitting under a tree. The purpose of Jehovah's unexpected coming is next revealed: he first tells Abraham that his aged wife Sarah shall bear him a son. Sarah laughs to herself on hearing this, which prompts a typically terse reaction from Jehovah:

> And the lord said unto Abraham, Wherefore did Sarah laugh, saying, Shall I of a surety bear a child, which am old? Is anything too hard for the Lord? At the time appointed I will return unto thee, according to the time of life, and Sarah shall have a son. (*Genesis* 18, vs. 13-14)

Jehovah and his companions next rise and look towards the town of Sodom, and Abraham, realising they intend going there, steps forward to show them the way. When they have together walked some distance, Jehovah halts with Abraham, while his two helpers continue on towards the town. Jehovah then tells Abraham that he is planning to destroy both Sodom and the nearby town of Gomorrah because he has heard that the sin of the inhabitants is 'very grievous', meaning it seems that they regularly engage in anal intercourse, both heterosexual and homosexual, which in the former case would have been used by the them as a method of birth control, hence our word 'sodomite'.

However, Jehovah continues by saying that he isn't entirely sure that the story is correct, which is why he must visit the town to find out the truth for himself. This of course means that Jehovah does not possess divine knowledge, as we might expect, but is instead reacting to rumour like an ordinary person. It also suggests he comes from a more advanced and presumably homophobic future society which has developed contraceptive techniques that render heterosexual anal intercourse unnecessary and which regards it as a repugnant and immoral activity.

A remarkable conversation then occurs between Jehovah and Abraham, for Abraham objects that a wholesale slaughter of all the inhabitants might mean that some innocent people will be killed, and respectfully asks: 'Shall not the Judge of all the earth do right?' Jehovah concurs, and says that he will spare Sodom if as few as fifty 'righteous' people can be found there. Having obtained his agreement on that, Abraham then wonderingly asks if he will spare it if forty-five, then if thirty, then if twenty, and finally if only ten non-practitioners of anal intercourse live there. Jehovah magnanimously agrees that he will, although he is not prepared to save Sodom if less than ten are found.

> And the Lord went his way, as soon as he had left communing with Abraham: and Abraham returned unto his place. (*Genesis*, 18, v. 33)

It seems entirely inexcusable for Jehovah to threaten to kill many thousands of people simply because they are doing something he does not agree with, and even more bizarre that it requires Abraham to point out the unfairness of him murdering the innocent along with the guilty. And we can't help wondering why, if he is the God he says he is, he neither knows the way to Sodom nor if the stories he has heard about its people are true, and why he does not divinely change the sodomitic behaviour he finds so reprehensible? His uncertainties and murderous threats belong more to an aging, angry and uptight time-slipping man than to a deity.

Jehovah's two assistants or 'angels' reach Sodom that evening, and meet up with a citizen called Lot outside its gates. Lot invites them into his house, which they enter after being persuaded by him to do so, and eat the meal he prepares. Not long afterwards other citizens of Sodom surround the house and demand that the strangers be delivered up unto them. Lot goes out and tries to reason with them, offering to send out his two virginal daughters if they will leave the men alone.

> And they said, Stand back. And they said again, This one fellow came in to sojourn, and he will needs be a judge: now we will deal worse with thee, than with them. And they pressed sore upon the man, even Lot, and came near to break the door. (*Genesis* 19, v. 9)

This passage is confusing, yet it seems to indicate that the 'one fellow (that) came in to sojourn, and he will needs be a judge' is Jehovah himself, who arrives after the two 'angels' and who has angered the citizens by both inquiring about, and criticising, their sodomitic habits. However, the 'angels' save Lot by pulling him into the house, and then themselves and possibly Jehovah as well by in some unexplained way blinding those outside (but see below for an explanation). Early next morning, at the angels' urging, Lot leaves Sodom with his wife and daughters, although his wife looks back at the subsequent destruction of the town, which Jehovah is hardly likely to have been responsible for, and is killed by being turned into a pillar of salt:

> Then the Lord rained upon Sodom and upon Gomorrah brimstone and fire from the Lord out of heaven. And he overthrew those cities, and all the plain, and all the inhabitants of the cities, and that which grew upon the

ground. (*Genesis* 19, vs. 24-5)

Such destruction originating from the sky is most likely to have been caused by the impact of a tolerably large meteorite, which could easily have caused the fiery damage described. Jehovah and his two assistants will have left Sodom beforehand, possibly along with Lot and his family.

The end of this strange story is as remarkable as its beginning. Lot and his two daughters flee to the nearby little town of Zoar, but Lot is afraid to remain there very long, and instead chooses to take refuge in a mountain cave. While living in the cave, his two daughters, in order to 'preserve' their father's seed, get him drunk and separately sleep with him on two successive nights, thereby becoming pregnant by him. Thus while many thousands die for practising contraceptive and homosexual sodomy, those who are spared commit what to us is the equally reprehensible if not worse act of incestuous intercourse. But then, as we have seen, incest was practised by several time-shifters in order to avoid breeding with the people of the time into which they come, and was apparently acceptable behaviour to them in the circumstances.

The next person to see and to speak with Jehovah is Abraham's son Isaac, who was not born until Abraham had reached the ripe old age of one hundred years (in 1896 BC). Many years later, a famine occurred in the land surrounding the town of Gerar, where Abraham and Isaac were then living, and Isaac went to speak with the Philistine king Abimelech about the situation, intending to travel on afterwards to Egypt. But before he could do this, he received an unexpected visitor:

> And the Lord appeared unto him, and said, Go not down into Egypt; dwell in the land which I shall tell thee of; sojourn in this land, and I will be with thee, and will bless thee; for unto thee, and unto thy seed, I will give all these countries, and I will perform the oath which I sware unto thy father Abraham . . . because that Abraham obeyed my voice, and kept my charge, my commandments, my statutes, and my laws. And Isaac

dwelt in Gerar. (*Genesis* 27, vs. 2-6)

It is regrettable that we are told nothing about the circumstances of this visitation, or about the appearance of Jehovah or what his voice sounded like, or about the apparent insouciance of Isaac in receiving it. This suggests that Isaac was approached by a man, not a manifesting deity, whose description his father must have often have told him about and whom he therefore accepted as someone who would offer him timely and sensible advice.

At Gehar Isaac and his men successfully re-dug several wells to provide themselves and their animals with water, which led to envy among, and disagreements with, the local Philistine herders, who increasingly regarded them as unwelcome interlopers. The strife between the two groups eventually forced Isaac with family, servants and animals to move about twenty miles further inland, to a place called Beer-sheba, which was hotter and drier, but where he found and re-dug several wells formerly dowsed and dug by his father Abraham.

Isaac's sojourn at Beer-sheba, which took place in the same year (probably 1804 BC), led to Jehovah appearing once again to him, in order to give him a short, reassuring message:

> And the Lord appeared unto him the same night, and said, I am the God of Abraham thy father: fear not, for I will be with thee, and will bless thee, and multiply thy seed for my servant Abraham's sake. (*Genesis* 26, vs. 24)

The brevity of what was said, particularly on this second occasion, surely means that Jehovah only returned from 'the future' with some difficulty to deliver it, and that he had trouble in maintaining the integrity of his physical state. Whole body time-slips, when they are not spontaneous, are evidently not easy to achieve, especially if two are made in quick succession from 'the future', as the pair made to Gerar and then Beth-sheba appear to have been.

The third man to have a direct contact with Jehovah was

the pastoralist Jacob, a son of Isaac. This resulted in a most curious encounter between the two men. At the time Jacob was trying to make peace with his agriculturalist fraternal twin brother Esau, both of whom were born in 1837 BC, and while on his way to meet Esau, accompanied by his family and their herds of cattle and other animals, they arrive at a river ford called Jabbok. It is there that Jacob, having sent his family and the beasts across the river ahead of him, has the following experience.

> And Jacob was left alone; and there wrestled a man with him until the breaking of the day. And when he saw that he prevailed not against him, he touched the hollow of his thigh; and the hollow of Jacob's thigh was out of joint, as he wrestled with him. And he said, Let me go, for the day breaketh. And he said, I will not let thee go, except thou bless me. And he said unto him, What is thy name? And he said, Jacob. And he said, Thy name shall be called no more Jacob, but Israel: for as a prince hast thou power with God and with men, and hast prevailed. And Jacob asked him, and said, Tell me, I pray thee, thy name. And he said, Wherefore is it that thou dost ask after my name? And he blessed him there. And Jacob called the name of the place Peniel: for I have seen God face to face, and my life is preserved. (*Genesis* 32, vs. 24-30)

This incident, which evidently occurred in 1739 BC, is not presented or meant as Jacob metaphorically 'wrestling with his conscience', but rather is portrayed as an actual wrestling contest between two men. And two very elderly men at that, as Jacob had then reached the age of ninety-eight years.

We can only wonder why Jehovah took part in it, unless of course wrestling was a sport that he practised in 'the future' and simply took the opportunity that Jacob presented him with to indulge in it. And Jacob is as good at wrestling as he is, if not better, which is why the encounter lasts for most of the night. This surely would not have been the case if Jehovah had been a real deity or a younger time-slipped man. Indeed, Jacob's ability to hold his own is recognised by

Stones at Bethel, where Jacob's wrestling match is said to have taken place.

Jehovah who gives him the new name (or rather title) of Israel, which means 'a prince of God'. Had the wrestling match merely been metaphorical or imaginary, then the use of the title Israel by Jacob would not only be entirely unjustified but would be little other than self-aggrandisement.

It is curious too why Jehovah does not tell Jacob, who specifically asks him, what his name is, or for that matter why he did not reveal it to Abraham or Isaac. Indeed, he keeps it secret for another two hundred and forty eight years, until 1491 BC, when he finally tells it to Moses, the son of Levi, whom he not only later assists in leading the Jews out of Egypt (where they have learned the basics of civilised life) but co-opts him into becoming his civilising agent by giving him the Ten Commandments along with a lot of other rules and regulations. Hence Jehovah may have adopted this uncharacteristic personal approach to encourage Moses to do what he asks of him.

> And God spake unto Moses, and said unto him, I am
> the Lord: And I appeared unto Abraham, unto Isaac,
> and unto Jacob, by the name of God Almighty, but by
> my name JEHOVAH was I not known to them . . .
> (*Exodus* 6, vs. 2 and 3),

But oddly, Jehovah keeps himself physically out of sight
within a dark cloud when he imparts the Ten
Commandments and other 'divers laws and ordinances' to
Moses on mount Sinai. Afterwards, however, he is not so
reticent, for he instructs Moses to descend from the
mountain, collect together Aaron, Nadab, and Adihu, and
seventy of the elders of Israel, and return with them. When
they arrive, Jehovah shows himself to them all:

> And they saw the God of Israel: and there was under his
> feet as it were a paved work of a sapphire stone, and as
> it were the body of heaven in his clearness. And upon
> the nobles of the children of Israel he laid not his hand:
> also they saw God, and did eat and drink. (*Exodus* 24,
> vs. 10-11)

There is no mistaking the described human form of Jehovah
in this passage. Furthermore, because eating is probably the
last thing that most people would think of doing if they
actually saw God, it is suggestive that Moses and his
companions both 'eat and drink' in the presence of Jehovah,
who would by then have been a most aged person. Jehovah's
growing sensitivity about his outward appearance explains
why when Moses later asks Jehovah if he might see him
again in the flesh, his request is only partially fulfilled:

> And he said, Thou canst not see my face: for there shall
> no man see me, and live. And the Lord said, Behold,
> there is a place by me, and thou shalt stand upon a
> rock: And it shall come to pass, while my glory passeth
> by, that I will put thee in a clift of the rock, and will
> cover thee with my hand while I pass by: And I will take
> away mine hand, and thou shalt see my back parts: but

my face shall not be seen. (*Exodus* 33, vs. 20-3)

We can only presume that this rear-view revealing takes place as it is not referred to again. Yet if it does, it is the fourth and last time that Jehovah actually shows his human form to anyone. This is not surprising in view of his great age. But clearly, those who believe that Jehovah is a human-shaped deity will accept that his face at least shines with such a glorious effulgence that it cannot be looked at without fatal consequences. Yet this cannot be so, as otherwise it would not only have destroyed Moses and his group earlier, but also Abraham, Isaac and Jacob. Anyhow, such a brightness would surely have been visible, and perhaps equally harmful, when he is seen from the rear.

None the less, while Jehovah and the other time-slippers are ordinary human beings, they all carry a very formidable weapon that has the shape of a staff, and which in the Old Testament is called the 'rod of God'. This was apparently an advanced technological device made partly of gold, which is so awe-inspiring that replicas were, and still are, carried by kings and emperors as symbols of their power and authority. We can only guess at the staff's internal structure or what forces it was capable of bringing to bear on those people or objects against whom or which it was used. Some of its powers were benign, such as those used by Hermes, while others, perhaps most, were highly dangerous and destructive. It could certainly generate some sort of heat-inducing ray like a laser, and we have an interesting example of one that was used by an 'angel' in this way to impress a man named Gideon:

> Then the angel of the lord put forth the end of his staff that was is in hand, and touched the flesh and the unleavened cakes; and there rose up a fire out of the rock, and consumed the flesh and the unleavened cakes.
> Then the angel of the Lord departed out of his sight. And when Gideon perceived that he was an angel of the Lord, Gideon said, Alas! O Lord God! for because I have seen an angel of the lord face to face. And the Lord said unto him, Peace be unto thee; fear not: thou shalt not

die. (*Judges* 7, vs. 1-3)

This passage likewise reveals there was nothing in the outward appearance of the 'angel' that was in any way different from that of an ordinary person; indeed, it was only after he had used his staff in such a dramatic fashion that Gideon realised he was one of Jehovah's assistants.

Moreover, while the rods were normally solid, they also had the capacity to become wholly flexible and, in this form, to exhibit some independent movement. And when necessary the time-slippers 'loaned' them to those with whom they were working, in order that they could defend themselves or produce stunning effects that would awe opponents into submission, or even destroy them.

The Old Testament records how in 1491 BC Jehovah gave Moses one of these 'magic' staffs in order that he might use it to persuade the Egyptian Pharaoh to free the Hebrews from their bondage. The Hebrews had migrated to Egypt in 1706 BC, after Joseph, the son of Jacob, had become the right-hand man of the Pharaoh, and under whose protection they had subsequently prospered and flourished. Joseph's rise to a position of power and influence in Egypt was engineered by Jehovah, who wanted the nomadic, animal-herding Hebrews admitted into the country in order that they would become exposed to, and thus learn about, civilised life. Then, when they had lived there for two hundred and fifteen years (during which period other important time-slipping missions were taking place in Greece and elsewhere), Jehovah decided they were sufficiently well-instructed in the physical aspects of civilisation to receive his special moral guidance, with which he was apparently obsessed. He was probably also concerned that the increasing antipathy shown by the Egyptians towards the Hebrews might threaten the entire mission.

The crucial meeting between Jehovah and Moses took place at Horeb, to where Moses had fled after having murdered an Egyptian he saw beating a fellow Hebrew. Jehovah spoke to him, so it is recounted, as a disembodied voice from the interior of the burning bush and told him that he was to lead the children of Israel out of Egypt to the promised land.

> And Moses answered and said, But, behold, they will not believe me, nor hearken unto my voice: for they will say, The Lord hath not appeared unto thee. And the Lord said unto him, What is that in thine hand? And he said, a rod. And he said, Cast it on the ground. And he cast it on the ground, and it became a serpent; and Moses fled from before it. And the Lord said unto Moses, Put forth thine hand, and take it by the tail. And he put forth his hand, and caught it, and it became a rod in his hand. (*Exodus* 4, vs 2-4)

This remarkable transformation of a rod into a serpent and back again cannot but remind us of the fact that the box containing Ra's deadly Uraeus, which is described as an asp (or serpent) that spat fire, also held Ra's rod or staff. Indeed, the two appliances were probably identical, the stiff rod-like one becoming, when the box was opened, a flexible asp-like one that shot out a consuming fire. If so, it may mean that the 'rod of God' retained its rod-like form when held but lost its stiffness and became, to all intents and purposes, a flexible, writhing object resembling a snake when thrown on the ground.

It may be objected that because Moses is presented as already possessing the rod when Jehovah spoke to him, it was not given to him by Jehovah but was instead an ordinary shepherd's staff. However, not long afterwards Jehovah says somewhat irritably to Moses, who had complained that he was not as fluent or as persuasive a speaker as his brother Aaron, that

> . . . he (i.e. Aaron) shall be thy spokesman unto the people: and he shall be, even he shall be to thee instead of a mouth, and thou shall be to him instead of God. And thou shall take this rod in thine hand, wherewith thou shalt do signs.' (*Exodus* 4, vs. 16, 17)

But clearly, Jehovah would have said ' take your rod' or 'take that rod' if he was referring to a rod owned by Moses, and not 'take this rod', which instead suggests he is referring to a rod that he has either just given him or was about to give him. This would also explain why the staff is called the 'rod of God' on subsequent occasions.

We can of course accept that if Jehovah was really a deity, he would be able to transform an ordinary wooden staff into not only a serpent and vice versa, but also into a weapon of great power; yet if instead he is, like the other 'gods' I have mentioned, a time-slipped person, then it is more likely that he presented Moses with a rod-shaped laser-like device, brought from 'the future', that could not only heat up and set fire to things but cause blindness when shone into people's eyes, as well as having far greater capabilities.

Soon afterwards Moses returned with his wife and sons to Egypt, with 'the rod of God in his hand'. There he managed to convince his fellow Hebrews that Jehovah had spoken to him, and they agreed to follow him and Aaron out of Egypt. But when Aaron asked the Pharaoh for permission to leave, it was refused. Jehovah then advised Aaron to 'take thy rod, and cast it before Pharaoh, and it shall become a serpent'.

> Then Pharaoh also called the wise men and the sorcerers: now the magicians of Egypt, they also did in like manner with their enchantments. For they cast down every man his rod, and they became serpents: but Aaron's rod swallowed up their rods. (Exodus, 7, vs. *11, 12*)

If Pharaoh's sorcerers were really able to magically transform their rods into serpents, it means that Jehovah's feat of apparently doing the same was not so marvellous after all. But such a transformation is more understandable if the sorcerers already possessed similar devices to Moses's 'rod of God' that lost their stiffness when cast upon the ground, which they may have done if they had inherited them from the time-travellers who had earlier visited Egypt. Also, it is difficult to understand how a real serpent could eat a number of others of approximately the same size, especially as snakes seldom, if ever, eat other snakes. But if the phrase 'swallowed up their rods' is a metaphor for Aaron's rod destroying those of Pharaoh's sorcerers, it suggests that his device, which is presumably the same 'rod of God', is actually more powerful than theirs.

Because Pharaoh refuses to change his mind about letting the people of Israel go, Moses is told by God to use 'the rod which was turned into a serpent' to change his mind, first by striking the waters of Egypt 'that they may become blood'.

> And Moses and Aaron did so, as the Lord commanded; and he lifted up the rod, and smote the waters that were in the river, in the sight of Pharaoh, and in the sight of his servants; and all the waters that were in the river were turned to blood. (*Exodus* 7, vs. *20*)

Indeed, the waters became undrinkable, the fish died, and the rivers stank. This is the first of the ten plagues of Egypt, half of which are brought about by the 'rod of God', for the Old Testament specifically states that either Moses or Aaron use the device to produce the next plague, that of frogs (2); then a plague of lice (3); severe hail (7); and a plague of locusts (8). Moses may also have used the rod to cause the ninth plague, a darkness lasting three days, although it is only recorded that he 'stretched forth his hand to heaven' to produce it. The other plagues, that of flies (4), cattle murrain (5), boils affecting both man and beast (6), and the death of Egypt's firstborn (10) are reportedly brought about directly by Jehovah.

After these dreadful visitations Pharaoh decides to let the Israelites go, and they were led by Jehovah, in the form of a cloud-like pillar, to the banks of the Red Sea. Yet Pharaoh, quickly regretting his decision, pursues them with his army in chariots, which frightened the fleeing Hebrews into thinking they would be trapped and killed. But the power of 'the rod of God' was again used to get them out of danger.

> And the Lord said unto Moses, Wherefore criest thou unto me? speak unto the children of Israel, that they go forward: But lift thou up thy rod, and stretch out thine

hand over the sea, and divide it: and the children of Israel shall go on dry ground through the midst of the sea. (*Exodus* 14, vs. 15-16)

The rod was held aloft by Moses and caused a strong wind to spring up that, by blowing all night, parted the Red Sea. Then once the Israelites had safely crossed the exposed bed of the river on foot, the rod was again used to close up the water, thereby drowning the entire Egyptian host that had recklessly tried to follow them. No mercy, as we might expect, was shown to the Egyptians by Jehovah!

Thus the Lord saved Israel that day out of the hand of the Egyptians; and Israel saw the Egyptians dead upon the sea shore. And Israel saw that great work which the Lord did upon the Egyptians: and the people feared the Lord, and believed in the Lord, and his servant Moses. (*Exodus* 14, vs. 30-31)

The Hebrews were then led by Moses into the hot, dry wilderness of the Sinai peninsula, which they had to cross to get to Canaan, the promised land. But despite the wonders they had already witnessed and their stated belief in Jehovah as God, it wasn't long before the parched desert conditions made them doubt that they had done the right thing. Many, in fact, wished themselves back in Egypt. Their hunger, however, was apparently quickly assuaged by Jehovah, who produced the nightly fall of a substance called manna, which the Hebrews collected from the ground every morning and on which they subsisted for their entire forty year stay in the desert. Now manna, both in its form, taste, and nutritive value, is identical to the substance called ambrosia eaten by the Greek 'gods', and thus appears to be the special food brought from 'the future' by the time-shifters.

But when the Hebrews next reached the desert of Sin they became parched due to the lack of water, and once more rail at Moses for bringing them into such a desolate place. Whereupon Moses, asking Jehovah what he should do, was told:

Behold, I will stand before thee upon the rock in Horeb; and thou shalt smite the rock (i.e. with the rod), and there shall come water out of it, that the people may drink. And Moses did so in the sight of the elders of Israel. (*Exodus* 17, v. 6)

Soon afterwards the 'rod of God' was again used by Moses when the Hebrews are threatened by some doughty desert warriors led by a man called Amalek.

And Moses said unto Joshua, Choose us out men, and go out, fight with Amalek: tomorrow I will stand on the top of the hill with the rod of God in mine hand . . . And it came to pass, when Moses held up his hand, that Israel prevailed: and when he let down his hand, Amalek prevailed. (*Exodus* 17, vs 9, 11)

On reaching mount Sinai, where the Hebrews set up camp, they are visited by the aged Jethro, who heard from his son-in-law Moses all about their escape from Egypt and the various tribulations they had successfully endured with the help of Jehovah. Jethro is understandably impressed, but his comments about Jehovah are none the less curious:

Now I know that the Lord is greater than all gods; for in the thing wherein they dealt proudly he was above them. (*Exodus* 18, v. 11)

Thus Jethro does not recognise Jehovah as the one True God, but simply as the greatest of several gods. And if the 'gods' he is referring to are time-slipping human beings, then we can understand what he means when he adds 'for in the thing wherein they dealt proudly he was above them'.

The arrival of the Hebrews at mount Sinai marks the climax of Jehovah's time-slipping mission. For atop the mountain he gives to Moses the enormous and all-encompassing body of 'divers laws and ordinances', part of which, namely the Ten Commandments, not only became the chief guide to right or moral behaviour for the Hebrews but also later for Christians and Moslems. We must therefore examine how these numerous laws and statutes were delivered to Moses.

Jehovah manifests, says the Old Testament, on the top of mount Sinai, which is covered with cloud, although it is unclear whether this is a natural cloud or one produced by him. He summons Moses up to meet him on the third day, when he gives to him the celebrated Ten Commandments and a mixed bag of other laws, which can be briefly summarised as: how to treat servants; the penalties for those committing manslaughter, theft, arson, cursing parents, harming pregnant women, stealing animals, etc.; how an injury caused must be punished by inflicting the same on the perpetrator; that widows, orphans and strangers must be treated with respect; that stray animals must be returned to their owners; that animals causing injury must be stoned to death; that those having sex with animals must be killed; that spreading false rumours must be avoided; that witches should be killed; that land must be left fallow in the seventh year; that no work is to be done on the seventh day; that no other gods are to be worshipped; and that three yearly feasts must be kept in honour of Jehovah.

Exodus 24, v. 4 says 'And Moses wrote all the words of the Lord' which suggests that he somehow took notes as Jehovah spoke, although elsewhere we are told that Jehovah gave Moses two tablets of stone with all the laws inscribed on them.

We know that Moses came down from the mount then, but returned there on the seventh day along with Aaron and the others, although because the cloud was present for only six days, the summit must have been clear when they did so, which presumably is why they all saw Jehovah. However, following the departure of his companions, Moses apparently remains there for forty days and nights, during which time he is given a set of detailed instructions for several articles that Jehovah wants the Hebrews to make, these being a) an ark of shittim or acacia wood; b) a table of shittim wood; c) a large tabernacle or tent; d) an altar of shittim wood; e) the court of the tabernacle; f) various priestly garments; g) several ouches or buckles of gold; and h) the breast-plate of judgment, plus instructions about how to kill, cook and serve a sacrificial bullock and ram. The articles are to be fashioned for both Jehovah's worship and convenience, as he intends to reside, so he says, in the tabernacle 'where I will meet you, to speak there unto thee. And there I will meet with the children of Israel, and the tabernacle shall be sanctified by my glory.'

We may reasonably wonder how Moses managed to survive on the top of mount Sinai for forty days and nights without food and water, and why, when he eventually descends, his face emits a noticeable and somewhat embarrassing glow, which obliges him to keep it covered with a cloth? I believe the probable answer to these questions is that Jehovah took Moses with him into 'the future', to his own time, where he was both given food and drink and the instructions mentioned above, while the facial glow he develops is a side-effect of his remarkable translocation there and back. The very elderly Jehovah would also need to obtain food for himself, avoid the bitter night-time cold, and presumably have the Ten Commandments and the other moral instructions 'laser-carved' into slabs of rock.

But alas, when Moses descends to the foot of the mountain, clasping the two tablets inscribed by the 'finger of God', he discovers to his horror that many of the Hebrews, having tired of waiting for him, have prevailed upon his friend Aaron to make them a golden calf out of their womenfolk's earrings, and are worshipping it by dancing around it with abandon. He is so shocked by their apostasy that he flings down the tablets and smashes them. Yet this is a scarcely believable act, for if Moses really believed that Jehovah is the True God, it is difficult to comprehend how he could have destroyed such precious objects. He deals, however, with the rebellious situation in a straightforwardly savage way. He discovers which Hebrews still believe in Jehovah, and tells them to put the calf-worshippers to the sword. They obey, and about three thousand of his fellows are thus murdered, although this cruel punishment is better than the one the angry Jehovah had intended to inflict on the Hebrews, which was to kill them all!

Jehovah then tells Moses that they should get ready to

depart from mount Sinai, and that he will send them an angelic guide to lead them 'unto a land flowing with milk and honey: for I will not go up in the midst of thee; for thou art a stiff-necked people: lest I consume thee in the way'. But first Moses erects the previously mentioned tabernacle or oblong-shaped Tent of Meeting some distance from the camp, outside the door of which Jehovah descends within a cloudy pillar.

> And all the people saw the cloudy pillar stand at the tabernacle door: and all the people rose up and worshipped, every man at his tent door. And the Lord spake unto Moses face to face, as a man speaketh to his friend. (*Exodus* 33, vs. 10-11)

But despite their 'face to face' proximity, Moses cannot see Jehovah within the dense cloud, which is why he asks 'if I have found grace in thy sight, shew me now thy way, that I may know thee'. This is when Jehovah, as mentioned above, refuses to reveal his face but says he will let Moses see his back parts instead.

Yet before any decampment is made by the Hebrews, Jehovah instructs Moses to carve out two new tablets of stone and then bring them to the top of the mountain. This Moses does, and Jehovah rewrites the Ten Commandments and the other lost laws on them. He also makes a covenant or agreement with Moses, to the effect that if the Hebrews continue to worship him and obey his laws, he will protect them and visit them regularly throughout their journey to Canaan. The visits are similarly accomplished by Jehovah descending into the tabernacle in a cloud, from within which he imparts dozens of extra laws and regulations to the ever-faithful and untiring Moses, all of which can be read in their tiresome prolixity in the Old Testament books of Leviticus, Numbers, and Deuteronomy.

The journey to Canaan takes forty years, throughout which Jehovah helps the Hebrews to overcome any local people that attack them, while maintaining a rigorous internal discipline among them by killing those who fail to do as he says. In particular, he strictly forbids the Hebrews from marrying outsiders, or from doing anything that might weaken their trust and belief in him, warning Moses that 'thou shalt worship no other god: for the Lord, whose name is Jealous, is a jealous god'.

We might also note that the two inscribed stone tablets are carried from place to place in the ark of the covenant, which is a rectangular chest made of acacia wood coated with gold, and which is carried on the shoulders of four or more men by means of two wooden gold-covered staves pushed through the metal rings, one at each of its upper corners. But the ark, which has a length of three foot nine inches, a width of two-foot three inches and a depth of the same size, is not merely a repository for Jehovah's laws written on stone, but can also emit a devastating fiery force that kills. And while we do not know if the 'rod of God', by also being placed within it, is responsible for its destructive powers, the ark is nonetheless remarkably similar to the box containing the fire-spitting Uraeus of Ra.

Jehovah continued to guide and exhort the Hebrews for several centuries afterwards, although he never again revealed himself in his human form as he had done to Abraham, Isaac, Jacob, Moses and the Hebrew nobles. His relationship with Moses and his followers was the most intimate, direct and important, providing as it did the Hebrews with the laws and customs that separated them from other races and the sense that they were a special or chosen people. But nonetheless, it is clear that Jehovah was not a deity but a man from 'the future', whose ability to return at different and often widely spaced dates enabled him to perform his functions as both a civiliser and protector for about one thousand years. He could do this by travelling back from his own time to contact them again at consecutively later dates in their history, to keep an eye on how they, as a people, were faring.

But then, like all the other time-shifters I have mentioned, his personal visits end. This probably happened because he aged to decrepitude and then died in his own time, which would explain why he did nothing to help them when they were persecuted and expelled from 'the promised land' by the Romans, and why he did nothing to quell their suffering much later on, which reached its ghastly climax in Nazi Germany.

Does this therefore mean, as Left-wing intellectuals were once fond of claiming, that God is dead? No, it most certainly does not. The early Hebrews, like the Egyptians, Sumerians, Greeks, Latins, Etruscans, Aztecs and other ancient peoples, were simply visited by time-slippers who came as civilisers and who either presented themselves as, or were considered to be, deities. But those contacted were not laughably wrong in believing as they did, for the time-shifters not only possessed apparent supernatural knowledge and power, but could also vanish and reappear, sometimes after long intervals, without change. Hence the contactees would have felt blessed indeed by the presence among them of such remarkable visitors, who gave so much that was beneficial and who asked for so little in return.

Yet the Eternal Oneness, the Supreme Being, is not a kindly middle-aged bearded man dressed in a long robe, comforting though this image is. It has no human, or even physical form. It exists as pure spirit, suffusing the entire universe and touching each and every part of it, knowing all that happens in this wonderful moment -- for that is all that it is -- we call time. It cannot ordinarily be perceived by our senses or understood by our thinking minds, yet it can still be experienced on occasions by those who actively seek its guidance and support. Indeed, many mystics have enjoyed a deep intimacy with the One.

Their meetings with the Eternal Oneness stand in complete contrast to those that Moses and his fellow Hebrews had with Jehovah. But if the reader still thinks that Jehovah and God are synonymous, I would ask him or her to consider this. Could a real divinity have given Moses Ten Commandments which include the injunction 'Thou shalt not kill' but then have had no compunction in slaughtering the many thousands of people living in Sodom and Gomorrah, as well as assisting Moses in bringing the ten plagues to Egypt which killed thousands more, in drowning the whole army of

Pharaoh, in organising the murder of three thousand of his own chosen people, and, later, in directing Joshua to overthrow and burn numerous cities in Canaan and to massacre all their occupants?

CHAPTER TEN

CONCLUSION

The splendours of the firmament of time
May be eclipsed, but are extinguished not:
Like stars to their appointed height they climb,
And death is a low mist which cannot blot
The brightness it may veil.

From *Adonais* by Percy Bysshe Shelley

I have examined some startling concepts and claims in the previous chapters, all of which are based on the proposition that time is not something that is passing us by in a linear fashion and which is neatly divided into a past that has gone for ever, a present that is, and a future that will be. Time in this sense is entirely the creation of our consciousness, which can normally only perceive, through our sense organs, individual 'moments' of the unity or Oneness, wherein all three parts, if we can call them that, simultaneously exist. If this were not the case time travel or time-slipping could not happen, contrary to the many instances of it which have been described.

Yet where in the Oneness, we may ask, are all those 'past' and 'future' moments and events in relation to ourselves? Could the Oneness really be like an enormous sausage through which we are slowly slicing our way, or is its internal structure quite different?

As we have seen, those who undergo a time-slip generally experience no physical movement but suddenly find themselves 'in' a different time, which in some cases is separated by millions of years from their own present. This suggests that the people, objects and events they witness occupy exactly the same position in space as themselves and must therefore somehow be interwoven with the seemingly solid, three-dimensional 'reality' in which they live. Or to put it another way, it means that not only are there dinosaurs walking through your living room as you read this book, but that every dinosaur -- like every other creature and object -- which ever occupied the space now taken by your living room is contained within it. The same applies to all those creatures, objects and events that are yet to occupy it.

However, the 'present moment' in which you and I apparently live is entirely the construct of our conscious minds, which they -- i.e. your consciousness and mine -- build up from the messages we receive from such receptor organs as the eye, the ear, the nose, etc. But the material world we see, hear, smell, touch and otherwise sense is made, as we know, from atoms, yet those atoms, and therefore ourselves, contain far more empty space than matter.

The proportion of each when compared is in the region of ten trillion to one, which means the objects around you, and you yourself, are ten trillion times less solid than you believe yourself and them to be. And even that slight solidity is illusory, as the 'matter' of an atom is not really there, for it is only an expression of the forces existing between sub-subatomic particles known as electrons, bosons and quarks, which themselves are quanta of energy. Hence we are all, one might say, shadows within a world of shadows.

Such an enormous preponderance of empty space means that it, and thus ourselves and the world around us, could easily be interpenetrated by atomic forces that are not, in this moment we call 'the present', capable of arousing perception in us, and which therefore, from our standpoint as conscious observers, do not exist. Indeed, we know that about ninety-five per cent of the 'matter' in the universe which should be there cannot be detected.

So where is it? It might perhaps invisibly interpenetrate our 'present' world and so form that part of the Oneness which we call 'the past' and 'the future'. If so, a time-slip, which is of course a misnomer because it doesn't normally shift anyone anywhere, results when someone is suddenly sensitised, for reasons which are not yet known, to a field of atomic force that constitutes a particular three-dimensional and equally 'real' scene, one that we interpret as belonging to either 'the past' or to 'the future'. Similarly, the 'whole body' Future or Past Encounter of the Fourth Kind must happen when a person's individual atomic force-field links up with, or joins with, that of the scene he or she witnesses, so enabling him or her to become a temporary (or possibly even a permanent) part of it.

Another well-attested example of the merging of two times happened not long after the first major battle of the English civil war, fought at Edgehill on 23 October 1642, which pitted the parliamentary army commanded by Robert Deveraux, Earl of Essex (1591-1646), against that led by King Charles I (1600-49). The battle was a very noisy affair involving as it did the shouts and screams of the combatants, the clash of swords and pikes, and the discharge of muskets and cannon.

Then in late December 1642 word reached King Charles that a strange re-enactment of the event had been heard and seen by several respectable residents of the nearby small town of Kineton. This prompted the king to send two trusted soldiers, a Colonel Kirke and a Captain Dudley, to investigate the reports. They arrived at Kineton on Saturday 6 January 1643, and learned from Richard Noakes, the keeper of the inn where they stayed, that both he and his wife had experienced and been frightened by the phenomenon three times previously, and soon afterwards that same evening they themselves heard the loud discharge of muskets and the roar of cannon.

The two soldiers, bracing themselves, mounted and rode their horses to the scene of the battle in which they had both fought, where to their amazement they witnessed men noisily fighting together, many of whom they recognised in the moonlight, and were felt by them as being solid, three-dimensional figures, who were thus as actively engaged in fighting as they had been on the day of the battle. Colonel Kirke actually took part in the battle again, and found himself shouting the 'same old orders' that he had on the day itself.

For this event was not a spectral re-enactment, despite the fear exhibited by their horses, because several of those they saw had, like themselves, survived the conflict. It was, rather, a merging of two times, wherein the 'past present' participated in by the two armies on 23 October 1642 merged with that of the 6 January 1643 'present' inhabited by Colonel Kirke and Captain Dudley, entering it like a bubble, to form a Past Present Encounter of the Third Kind.

Charles I, King of England

It has been said that the universe is an idea in the 'mind' of God. But the Oneness itself is God, from whom, as the source of consciousness, we derive our ability to participate in it. And because there is more than 'one idea' in the Oneness, which contains all possibilities, there must be an almost infinite number of other dimensions as well. Thus not only are there worlds which parallel our own, but there must also be variants of it, wherein we are able to follow life routes that are closed to us, for one reason or another, in this one. Indeed, I have mentioned other people who appear to have been time-slipped into one of these variants. Hence while our individual 'time line' in this dimension is complete in itself and thus pre-ordained, it may be possible to take an alternative route at particular 'time line' crossroads, and thus, in this way, to change 'the future'.

Who, then, were the time-slipping civilisers and from where did they come? Why did they do what they did? And why, from their point of view, was their mission a disastrous failure?

Their tall, fair-skinned physical type indicates a Northern Hemisphere origin, with either Europe or western Russia being the likeliest site of their homeland. However, it is impossible to locate it with any degree of accuracy because they do not now belong to our 'time line'.

Their society, as we have noted, does not seem to have been a very advanced one, judging it by the simple agricultural, metal-working, corn-grinding, brick-making, stone-working, cloth-making and other handicrafts they taught, or by the few implements like the ox-drawn plough, pickaxe, hoe, adze and axe they introduced to the peoples whom they visited; yet against this we must set their staff or rod of God, which implies their possession of a sophisticated technology.

They were also talented builders, and the writing they imparted to the Egyptians was a clever mixture of signs and symbols, known as hieroglyphs. And they were probably limited in what they could bring with them, for while a time-slip was able to transport them, their clothes and their staves into a 'past present,' it might not have been able to do the same with any of their more cumbersome appliances.

We must also recognise that, if we were able to mount a similar time-slip mission, it would probably be counter-productive to transport, say, tractors, combine harvesters, crop-sprayers and all the other technological paraphernalia of present-day farming back to Neolithic times, because not only would most of it be quite unsuitable for the land conditions encountered, but the people themselves would be quite unable to use it; and they would probably be scared out of their wits by it.

Hence the activity of time-slip visitors would have been curtailed in this way, or, instead, be part of a carefully thought-through strategy to introduce easy-to-grasp techniques and easy-to-handle tools that could be used, and eventually manufactured by, those they came among.

None the less, they do appear to have possessed developed psychic powers, as a use of telepathy would explain their apparent knowledge of local languages, for by establishing a direct mind-to-mind link with those with whom they conversed, each would seemingly comprehend the others' spoken words. Such abilities would also have heightened their god-like status. Moreover, in some cases they were sufficiently alike to the indigenes to be their genetic descendants, and thus to possibly have a direct knowledge of their tongue.

They were said to be highly skilled at 'magic', and they were certainly able to do a number of things that seem miraculous even today, such as healing the sick and reanimating corpses. These were probably brought about by using presently unknown or forgotten medical treatments or by using psychic healing, both of which would have seemed magical to the people concerned. They also brought with them, as iterated above, a compact, advanced weapons' system which resembled a staff or rod, and they perhaps made more of these remarkable devices after their arrival. The staves were sometimes kept in a special box, apparently for reasons of safety. Some time-slip visitors could also produce dense clouds to hide themselves in when necessary, and possibly make fire fall from the sky.

Their humanity is further revealed by their inability to wholly protect themselves against the diseases they encountered, and by the fact that they could suffer injury and were not unaffected by ageing and death. They likewise had normal sexual desires. They had a loathing of polygamy and of buggery, yet found incest acceptable. They practised male circumcision, which they introduced to both the Egyptians and the Hebrews, among others. And they did not tolerate cannibalism.

They understood that civilised societies can only develop within a framework of law, which is why they introduced a code of law to those they visited. This aspect of their work was made the focal point of the mission conducted by Jehovah, who had an almost unhealthy obsession with rules and regulations. Hence their own society probably had a similar moral and legal infrastructure that helped mould their behaviour.

But none the less, some did not think twice about killing those who might obstruct their work, which suggests they believed the end justifies the means; and the end, in their case, were the benefits their own society, as they surmised, would inherit from the introduction of civilisation to earlier and more backward forebears.

It has been repeatedly said that they came from 'the future' yet they seemingly did not come from our 'future'. It was rather 'the future' as it originally existed for the people of 'the past' whom they contacted. For while the time-slipping first-comers carefully avoided mating with those 'past present' natives they met in order to avoid introducing biological 'loose cannons' into their past, their descendants failed to adhere to this strict policy.

And it was in this and in other ways that they fell into a trap of their own making. After all, their 'future' society had come into existence by the slow process of gradual social evolution, yet when they prematurely introduced civilisation to the Neolithic hunter-gatherers living two or more centuries before their time, they inadvertently caused such an accelerated rate of change, with an accompanying explosion of population growth, that both they and their society were wiped out by it -- both simply failed to evolve as they had done, which explains of course why they no longer visit us.

Or we can perhaps more accurately say that by their actions the time-shifters directed 'us' into another time line, one that does not include them, for they would have become the victims of what can be called the Patricide Paradox. To understand this imagine, for example, that a modern time-shifter went back to the year before he was born and inadvertently killed his own father. By doing so, he would simultaneously destroy himself because, with his father dead, he could not be conceived. Yet if he could not be conceived, his father could not be killed by him. Therefore his parent could in fact father him, and so the cycle -- known as a 'time loop' -- would repeat itself, *ad infinitum.*

The luckless time-shifters, who hoped to take advantage of their extraordinary discovery, may in fact have locked themselves into a similar closed system, which therefore terminates their particular time line at the point where they began their civilising missions into 'the past'. But -- and this is the good bit -- the Patricide Paradox also means that they will keep opening new time lines identical to ours, parallel worlds in fact, which contain not simply replicas of you and me, but real living people who are as much you and I as we are!

Hence we are not alone in our trials, tribulations and joys, but probably have numerous 'time twins' whose lives exactly mirror our own. Let us help make them happy by being kind, positive, caring and loving ourselves, and to remember, as Shelley wrote:

> All things that we love and cherish,
> Like ourselves must fade and perish;
> Such is our rude mortal lot –
> Love itself would, did they not.

THE END

SHORT BIBLIOGRAPHY

Borrow, George, *The Bible in Spain* (John Murray, 1869)

Bray, Warwick, and Trump, David, *The Penguin Dictionary of Archaeology* (Penguin Books, 1973)

Carrington, Hereward, *Psychic Oddities* (Rider and Company, 1952)

Childe, V. Gordon, *Man Makes Himself* (Watts & Co., 1941)

Cockell, Jenny, *Past Lives, Future Lives* (Piatkus Books, 1996)

Coleman, Dr Michael H. (editor),*The Ghosts of the Trianon* (The Aquarian Press, 1988)

Corliss, William R., *The Unexplained: A Sourcebook of Strange Phenomena* (Bantam Books, 1976)

Creighton, Helen, *Bluenose Ghosts* (McGraw-Hill Ryerson Limited, 1976)

Davidson, H. R. Ellis, *Gods and Myths of Northern Europe* (Penguin Books, 1974)

Durant, G. M., *Journey into Roman Britain* (G. Bell & Sons, Ltd.,1957)

Dyall, Valentine, *Unsolved Mysteries* (Hutchinson, 1954)

Emery, Walter B., *Archaic Egypt* (Penguin Books, 1961)

Forman, Joan, *The Masks of Time* (MacDonald and Jane's, 1978)

Frankfort, Henri, et al, *Before Philosophy: The Intellectual Adventure of Ancient Man* (Penguin Books, 1973)

Goddard, Sir Victor, *Flight Towards Reality* (Turnstone Books, 1975)

Goudge, Elizabeth, *The Joy of the Snow* (Hodder and Stoughton, 1974)

Happold, F. C., *Mysticism, A Study and an Anthology* (Penguin Books, 1963)

Hooke, S.H., *Middle Eastern Mythology* (Penguin Books, 1975)

Hutton, Bernard J., *Out of This World* (Psychic Press Ltd.)

Diagram Visual Information Ltd., *A Field Guide to Dinosaurs* (Avon Books, 1983)

Larousse Encyclopedia of Mythology (Batchworth Press Limited, 1959)

Lempriere, J., DD, *A Classical Dictionary* (George Routledge and Sons, 1919)

Marsh, Henry, *The Caesars* (David & Charles, 1972)

Martin, M., *A Description of the Western Isles of Scotland*, 1703

Michell, John, and Richard, Robert, *Phenomena: A Book of Wonders* (Thames and Hudson, 1977)

Parker, Henry Michael Deane, *A History of the Roman World From AD 138 to 337* (Methuen & Co. Ltd., 1958)

Pausanias, *Guide to Greece*, Volume 1 (Penguin Classics, 1979)

Picken, Stuart D. B., *The Soul of an Orkney Parish* (The Kirkwall Press, 1972)

Priestley, J. B., *Man and Time* (Aldus Books Limited, 1964)

Prescott, William H., *History of the Conquest of Mexico* (George Routledge and Sons, Ltd., 1901)

Reader's Digest Mysteries of the Unexplained (Reader's Digest Association Inc., 1982)

Reeves, The Reverend William, *Ecclesiastical Antiquities of Down, Connor, and Dromore* (Hodge and Smith, Dublin, 1847)

Smith, William, and Cheetham, Samuel, *A Dictionary of Christian Antiquities* (Kraus Reprint Co., 1968)

Stace, Walter C., *The Teachings of the Mystics* (Mentor Books, 1960)

Steiger, Brad, *Mysteries of Time and Space* (Sphere Books, 1977)

Suetonius, *The Twelve Caesars* (Penguin Classics, 1957)

Verril, Alpheus Hyatt, *Secret Treasure* (D. Appleton and Company, 1931)

Wilson, Colin, and Grant, John, *Mysteries* (Chancellor Press 1994)

Wood-Martin, William G., *Traces of the Elder Faiths in Ireland* (Longmans, Green and Co., 1902)

INDEX

ABOUT THE AUTHOR

Rodney Davies has written about the paranormal and strange occurrences for over thirty years, and he is now one of the best-known authors in the field. After graduating from university, he taught biology before joining a Montreal publishing company to begin his literary career. He has had eighteen books published, several of which have become best-sellers

Printed in Great Britain
by Amazon